THE LIGHT AND THE ROCK

THE LIGHT
AND THE ROCK
THE VISION OF *Dag Hammarskjöld*

EDITED BY T. S. SETTEL

E. P. Dutton & Co., Inc.   New York   1966

INTRODUCTION

"The road inwards," Dag Hammarskjöld once said, "can become a road outwards. For the traveller with open eyes and alert senses, the outward road can in a deeper sense become a road home." The publication in 1964 of *Markings,* a private notebook kept for many years by the late Secretary-General of the United Nations, astonished many readers for its revelation of "the road inwards" that Dag Hammarskjöld had so long explored. Those who knew the great statesman well, however, were not surprised by *Markings* or the key it provided to an understanding of its author: the ideas expressed in it are everywhere apparent in his public speeches and writings.

The purpose of *The Light and the Rock* is to show that the inward road was made evident in the outward road. *The Light and the Rock* is, like *Markings,* a collection of very brief statements which reflect Dag Hammarskjöld's innermost thoughts and beliefs of the condition of man, of nations, and of the hope for international cooperation and understanding. It is, in the most comprehensive sense of the word, an inspirational book. In it the late Secretary-General speaks his mind about problems of the utmost concern to us all: maturity, responsibility, the life of the man of public service, the conditions and obligations of freedom, religion, art, literature, history, the precise observation of the natural world. As one would expect, he has a great deal to say about the development of society and the role of the United Nations in maintaining world peace.

It is difficult, perhaps impossible, to arrive at a satisfactory understanding of Hammarskjöld's personality. His most intimate friends differ in their evaluation of his character. One can only approach him through the words he spoke and wrote. In these he revealed erudition and a vast range of interests. An examination of his personal library contains a few clues: there are books on the religion of the ancient Hindus, the Far Eastern cults, and Indian folklore. There are books on Christianity, Judaism and Mohammedanism. There are books by Dale Carnegie, Walter Lippmann, George Bernard Shaw, James Jones, Irwin Shaw, and a number of books about Lincoln and Schweitzer.

The material in *The Light and the Rock* was selected from a staggering quantity of papers left by Hammarskjöld. All of it is drawn from the public record. The editor wishes to express gratitude to the members of the staff of the United Nations Library who graciously opened their bookshelves and files for research. To the family and friends of Dag Hammarskjöld and the Royal Library in Stockholm, the editor is most grateful for the many courtesies extended in our quest for material for this book. Thanks also go to Carol Andren who translated much Swedish material.

T. S. SETTEL

TABLE OF CONTENTS

 # Part I

THE INDIVIDUAL
THE INDIVIDUAL AND SOCIETY

Fear motivates much of human action. It is our worst enemy and, somehow, seems to taint at least some corner of the heart of every man.

We all know how, when moved by fear, people may act against what others see as their own best interest. We know how, when people are afraid, they may act even against their own fundamental will. We have seen how, when influenced by such actions, the course of events may take on aspects of inexorable futility to the point where, out of sheer weariness, no resistance to the gravitation into open conflict any longer seems possible. This is a constantly repeated pattern of tragedy.

I suppose that, just as the first temptation of the realist is the illusion of cynicism, so the first temptation of the idealist is the illusion of Utopia.

Conflicts in human life are often never resolved, but simply outgrown.

If a mountain wall is once climbed, later failures do not undo the fact that it has been shown that it can be climbed.

. . . There is one thing that nobody ever needs to lose, and that is his self-respect.

It may be said that no man is neutral in the sense that he is without opinions or ideals.

A self-knowledge may expand the understanding of other people's worlds.

If I look back at the results of my intense interest in photography, it is less the pictures I have taken than how I, through them, learned how to see what is of importance.

We cannot mold the world as masters of a material thing. But we can influence the development of the world from within as a spiritual thing.

. . . Those who feel they had to sacrifice to maintain principle may be the first to profit from the fact that the principle was maintained. As individuals we know that the law which restrains us likewise protects us.

As individuals, we can put our influence on the side of what we believe is right and true. We can help in the movement toward those ends that inspire our lives and are shared by all men of good will.

The road inwards can become a road outwards. For the traveler with open eyes and alert senses, the outward road can in a deeper sense become a road home.

In the flourishing literature on the art of life there is much talk about that rare quality: maturity of mind. It is easy to circumscribe such maturity in negative terms. In positive terms it is difficult to define it, although we all recognize it when we have the privilege of seeing its fruits. It is reflected in an absence of fear, in recognition of the fact that fate is what we make it. It finds expression in an absence of attempts to be anything more than we are, or different from what we are, in recognition of the fact that we are on solid ground only when we accept giving to our fellow men neither more nor less than what is really ours.

·   ·   ·

There is no formula to teach us how to arrive at maturity and there is no grammar for the language of inner life.

The ways that we learn in childhood are only very meagerly adequate to the issues that we must meet in maturity.

The dignity of man, as a justification for our faith in freedom, can be part of our living creed only if we revert to a view of life where maturity of mind counts for more than outward success and where happiness is no longer to be measured in quantitative terms.

A mature man is his own judge. In the end, his only form of support is being faithful to his own convictions. The advice of others may be welcome and valuable, but it does not free him from responsibility. Therefore, he may become very lonely. Therefore, too, he must run, with open eyes, the risk of being accused of obdurate self-sufficiency.

It is a common experience to everyone who has tried to pursue a line of independence and objectivity in human affairs that he comes under criticism from those who believe that they would have had a greater chance of success for their own special aims, if it had not been for his attitude.

What experience does the passenger on a steamship get from the sea compared to that of a sailor? The esthetical viewing of a landscape served on a tray from a hotel terrace or during a plane trip will soon fade and weigh lightly compared to the picture we get when the experience is gained step by step, with knit muscles and open minds.

What is true in a life of action, like that of a politician or a diplomat, is true also in intellectual activities. Even a genius never achieves a lasting result in science without patience and hard work, just as in politics the results of the work of the most brilliant mind will ultimately find their value determined by character. Those who are called upon to be teachers or leaders may profit from intelligence, but can only justify their position by integrity.

It is false pride to boast to the world about the importance of one's work, but it is false humility and finally just as destructive not to recognize—and recognize with gratitude—that one's work has a sense.

Certainly, words about the evil of the day and the things of the morrow mean that our actions should be guided by a thoughtful and responsible consideration of future consequences of what we do. They mean that our life should be pursued with the patience of one who has no anxiety about results, acting in the calm self-surrender of faith.

Politics and diplomacy are no play of will and skill where results are independent of the character of those engaging in the game. Results are determined not by superficial ability, but by the consistency of the actors in their efforts and by the validity of their ideals. Contrary to what seems to be popular belief, there is no intellectual activity which more ruthlessly tests the solidity of a man than politics. Apparently, easy successes with the public are possible for a juggler, but lasting results are achieved only by the patient builder.

Faced with the worlds of others, one learns that he who has fully absorbed what his own world has to offer is best equipped to profit by what exists beyond its frontiers. Nothing is more natural.

· · · ·

Is it not our profound childhood familiarity with the fields and forests round the corner from our own house which enables us to move with assurance on the soil of others? Is it not on the basis of a deeper feeling for, and insight into our mother tongue that we learn to speak other languages most easily?

· · · ·

We travel to other countries and other parts of the world. Perhaps we experience the overwhelming grandeur of the Asiatic mountain ranges, the unearthly quiet of the African deserts, the South American rain forests or Polynesia's water regions. We meet people of other races and other faiths. But the more we see and the wider our contact with people in other parts of the world becomes, the clearer it is to us that the essential impressions of beauty and the final human values are as present among "the rocks where as children we played" as in these other far larger worlds.

· · · ·

"Know your country"—the formula was directly linked to the famous classical maxim. It demonstrates that the knowledge sought was seen as a way to increase knowledge of oneself. As always, and in all contexts, such a knowledge to oneself can widen the understanding of the worlds of others. In such a situation, the road chosen appeared as a road ahead. But it was also a road that led inwards. Therefore, it could in the end become a road outwards. "Know your country" meant both "Know yourself" and "Know your world." Thus interpreted, the slogan excluded just as emphatically both an empty internationalism and a narrow isolation within the limited confines of the homeland.

The world in which I grew up was dominated by principles and ideals of a time far from ours and, as it may seem, far removed from the problems facing a man of the middle of the twentieth century. However, my way has not meant a departure from those ideals. On the contrary, I have been led to an understanding of their validity also for our world of today. Thus, a never abandoned effort, frankly and squarely to build up a personal belief in the light of experience and honest thinking has led me in a circle; I now recognize and endorse, unreservedly, those very beliefs which were once handed down to me.

All of us, in whatever field of intellectual activity we work, influence to some degree the spiritual trend of our time. All of us may contribute to the breakdown of the walls of distrust and toward checking fatal tendencies in the direction of stale conformism and propaganda. How can this be done better or more effectively than by simple faithfulness to the independence of the spirit and to the right of the free man to free thinking and free expression of his thoughts?

We give to our daily work what it is in our power to give, when we meet the demands facing us to the full extent of our ability. This will ultimately lead us to greater justice and good will, even if nothing would seem to give us hope of success or even of progress in the right direction.

The Bhagavad Gita echoes somewhere an experience

of all ages and all philosophies in these words: "Work with anxiety about results is far inferior to work without such anxiety, in calm self-surrender." These are words of worldly wisdom which we can all share.

Leadership, the word I have used to designate what may come instead of superior power, is a dangerous word if one does not keep in mind that the most influential leaders in the European cultural evolution were askers of questions, like Socrates or the carpenter's Son from Nazareth.

. . . .

It is a sign of the highest culture to be really capable of listening, learning, and therefore also responding in a way which helps the less favored ones. It is a privilege reserved for the half-educated who is unaware of his limitations to be a poor listener in a feeling of his own false superiority.

Love should mean simply an overflowing of the strength with which we feel ourselves filled when living in true self-oblivion. And this love finds natural expressions in an un-hesitant fulfillment of duty and in an unreserved acceptance of life, whatever it brings us personally of toil, suffering—or happiness.

. . . .

From generations of soldiers and government officials on my father's side, I inherited a belief that no life was more satisfactory than one of selfless service to your country—or humanity. This service required a sacrifice of all personal inter-ests, but likewise the courage to stand up unflinchingly for your convictions.

In looking back to find a situation reflecting the essen-tial core of my father, Hjalmar Hammarskjöld's personality, I pause before this recollection.

It is late in the day, the third day of the defense debate of 1925. In the First Chamber, the discussion has largely been colored by echoes from the great battles of 1914. Hjalmar Hammarskjöld, who has sharply fought for his views from his position outside the parties, has become a personal target. In this situation he takes the floor for the last time. He ends with these words: "It was said here, before the recess, that large circles realized that in the question of defense, they could follow no poorer counsellor than I. To the extent that this is true, I would ask you gentlemen all to forget, and forget completely, that I am a friend of strong defenses, so as to prevent this from being an obstacle to a good decision. Who takes the initiative, who exerts influence, is so utterly indifferent compared to the one great question: to make our country secure for the future."

To me, a nineteen-year-old listener in the gallery, these words epitomized a life of faith in justice and of self-effacing service under a responsibility which unites us all.

．．．．

In 1930, Hjalmar Hammarskjöld left his post as Governor. The final period of his life thus begun was as long as the whole of his gubernatorial term. It covers the upsurge of Nazism, the Second World War and the Cold War. In spite of further public tasks, and in spite of an intense interest in what happened throughout the period, he was a man placed entirely aside. Sometimes he reflected resignedly on the extravagance of life, which constantly shoved aside the experience built over long years, finally to let it be destroyed by senescence and death.

．．．．

While my father, Hjalmar Hammarskjöld, unhesitatingly embraced the standpoint of justice, he knew full well how incomplete and fluid were the rules in which the idea of justice was reflected in international intercourse. It was certainly not his view that a small country like Sweden had to strive to save them for a coming era of peace even at the cost of vital interests of her own; the point might be reached when compromises became as natural for a neutral state as for a belligerent. But until such a situation arose, the neutral had particular obligations toward the future.

．．．．

. . . The empty chair was turned outward, toward Humlegarden Park, where the swarms of jackdaws prepared to retire for the night into the autumn-reddened trees around the Royal Library. Those swarms of jackdaws, whose seemingly senseless fighting my father had followed during his last years with ironical amusement, presented to him a picture of the rage of the heathen and the vain imaginings of the people. More and more in his loneliness, he longed for those swarms of jackdaws, and greeted them as messengers from the fields and spires in the Upsala of his youth and manhood.

In the stillness around this final station of my father's path, one remembers his childhood home in the Småland forests, on the border of Östergötland, more than ninety years ago. My father was one of those men who are firm in their roots and firm in their faith. He was one of those whose changing fates may well deepen the convictions and directions of their early years, but not change them. They may be transported far from their original setting, but their roots are never cut off. In that sense, his life ended where it began.

· · · ·

He achieved an inner unity because, in the period of revolutionary development through which he lived, he remained faithful to his past, and faithful also to the past of others. By easily discernible intermediate stages, this faithfulness bridged the span to a far earlier era, seventeenth-century Sweden, when the throne, the altar and the sword formed a terse triad in which a nation found its melody. Did that mean that he belonged to the past? Were his reactions to the problems of the day "a cold and bitter gust from times gone by," as an adversary whom he held in high esteem once said in a stormy political debate during the 1920's? Everyone must decide for himself what is the right answer, but fairness requires that it be based on knowledge. A man of firm convictions does not ask, and does not receive understanding from those with whom he comes into conflict. In the synthesis which should be the task of posterity, it is necessary to disengage oneself from earlier conflicts to examine what he really stood for, and judge the power of survival of these things without projecting the conflicts of our day into the past.

. . . The explanation of how man should live a life of active social service in full harmony with himself as a member of the community of the spirit, I found in the writings of those great medieval mystics for whom "self-surrender" had been the way to self-realization, and who in "singleness of mind" and "inwardness" had found strength to say yes to every demand which the needs of their neighbors made them face, and to say yes also to the very fate life had in store for them when they followed the call of duty, as they understood it.

In my official capacity, the private man should disappear and the international public servant take his place. The public servant is there in order to assist those who make the decisions which frame history. He should—as I see it—listen, analyze and learn to understand fully the forces at work and the interests at stake, so that he will be able to give the right advice when the situation calls for it. Don't think that he—in following this line of personal policy—takes but a passive part in the development. It is a most active one. He is active as an instrument, a catalyst, an inspirer.

The greatest contribution to international life that anyone can render—is to represent frankly and consistently what survives or emerges as one's own. Far from demanding that we abandon or desert ideals and interests basic to our personality, international service thus puts us under the obligation to let those ideals and interests reach maturity and fruition in a universal climate.

The principle of justice can be regarded as flowing naturally from the principles of equal political rights and equal economic opportunities. It has deep roots in the history of the efforts of man to eliminate from international life the anarchy which he had already much earlier overcome on the national level, deeper indeed than the political and economic principles which, as is well known, were much later to get full acceptance also in national life.

Interpreted in a broad sense, "the pursuit of equality at home and abroad" reflect a basic human right, equal in significance to the right to security and freedom from fear.

If, at long last, the recognition of human dignity means to give others freedom from fear, then that recognition cannot be simply a question of passive acceptance. It is a question of the positive action that must be taken in order to kill fear.

This is not a question of abstract ethical principles. I state conclusions from some very concrete recent experiences. It is when we all play safe that fatality will lead us to our doom. It is in the dark shade of courage alone, that the spell can be broken.

. . . .

What is the right to security? Is it not the right to the free development of individual and national life within the limits set by the right of other parties to the same security? What is the right of freedom from attack? Is it not the right to freedom from fear?

Thus we see how close the links are between the philosophy reflected in the recognition of the rights of individuals and the basic principles which may decide the issue of war and peace.

Lasting peace is not possible without recognition of fundamental human rights and human rights cannot reach their full development unless there is peace.

. . . .

The work for peace must be animated by tolerance and the work for human rights by respect for the individual. A student of the growth of human rights through the ages will recognize this close relationship to the development of tolerance inspired by intellectual liberalism, or perhaps, more often, by ethical concepts of religious origin. Attempts are made to link the development of human rights exclusively to the liberal ideas which broke through to predominance in the Age of Enlightenment. However, to do so means to overlook the historical background of those ideas. It means also cutting our ties to a source of strength that we need, in order to carry the work for human rights to fruition and to give to those rights, when established, their fitting spiritual content.

. . . .

We know that the question of peace and the question of human rights are closely related. Without recognition of human rights we shall never have peace, and it is only within the framework of peace that human rights can be fully developed.

In fact, the work for peace is basically a work for the most elementary of human rights: the right of everyone to security and to freedom from fear. We, therefore, recognize it as one of the first duties of a government, to take measures in order to safeguard for its citizens that very right. But we also recognize it as an obligation for the emerging world community to assist governments in safeguarding this elementary human right without having to lock themselves in behind the wall of arms.

Why is war and fear of war in the headlines of every daily paper if not because man fears man and nation, nation? Could there be a more eloquent sign of how far we are from recognition of the philosophy behind the principles of human rights, on which alone peace can be built? Can there be a greater challenge for us to work for a recognition of the dignity of man which would eliminate the fear that is eating our world like a cancer?

Both the work for peace and the work for human rights must be anchored in and inspired by a general approach which gives balance and substance to the results. Peace cannot be enforced for selfish reasons. Equality cannot be imposed as an abstract concept. In fact, attempts to do so account for some of the darkest episodes in history.

The development of society is such that in the very interest of the individual, the organized collectivity can no longer give the same scope to individual action as was possible in a smaller and less developed community. Modern man seldom acts alone. He is integrated in a series of collectivities which together form our society. In almost every phase of his life and work, he feels the necessity of organizing his activities in common with others. Over and above these various collectivities, the individual meets the state—and beyond the state there is the international community of nations with its necessarily ever-widening influence.

The conflict between different approaches to the liberty of man and mind, and between the different views of human dignity and the right of the individual, is continuous. The dividing line goes within ourselves, within our own peoples, and also within other nations. It does not coincide with any political or geographical boundaries. The ultimate fight is one between the human and the subhuman. We are on dangerous ground if we believe that any individual, any nation or any ideology has a monopoly on rightness, liberty and human dignity.

When we fully recognize this and translate our insight into

words and action, we may also be able to re-establish full human contact and communications across geographical and political boundaries.

We hear much about freedom and the blessings of freedom. We hear less about the obligations of freedom and the ideals by which freedom must be guided. Every individual prefers freedom from constraint and freedom from intervention in his personal pursuit of happiness. But, as we all recognize, such freedom is possible in a world of order only when the individual replaces outward limitations on his freedom of action by self-imposed laws which may be, and frequently are, no less severe. An individualism, carried to the extreme, where you neither accept restraint imposed on you by society, nor submit yourself to the laws of a mature conscience, would lead to anarchy.

The last half century has brought to fruition, with revolutionary consequences, ideas and initiatives of generations. The change is in no way complete; we are perhaps only at its beginning. The final results are still undetermined, but, to a large extent, will be decided by our way of reacting to the developing situation.

In very simple words, one of the leading nuclear physicists has formulated our personal problem when he says that the ways that we learned in our childhood are now only very meagerly adequate for the issues that we must meet in maturity. His words stress how developing knowledge and technology, and a developing society, require of us a continuous development also of the individual.

There has been an awakening to a living sense of heritage and resources, and to a healthy pride in the awareness of one's individuality, regarded not as a limitation but as an asset. That which is one's very own is experienced not as something provincial on the outskirts of the world, but as an essential part of the resources humanity as a whole has to manage.

The pursuit of happiness, under laws of conscience, alone can justify freedom. It is part of the American creed, part of the inherited ideology of all Western civilization, that each man is an end in himself, of infinite value as an individual. In the fight for freedom, which puts its stamp so strongly on present-day life, the final issue is what dignity we are willing to give to man. But what is, in fact, the central tenet of this ideology becomes a reality only when we, ourselves, follow a way of life which entitles us personally to the freedom of a mature individual, living under the rules of his conscience. And it becomes the key to our dealings with others, only when inspired by a faith which in truth and spirit gives to them the value which is theirs according to what we profess to be our creed.

. . . .

In the world of today, there is an urge to conformism. This sometimes makes people complain of a lack of loyalty in those who criticize the attitudes prevalent in their environment. May I ask: Who shows true loyalty to that environment? Is it the one who in his own conscience has arrived at the conclusion that something is wrong, and in all sincerity gives voice to his criticism, or the one who, in self-protection, closes his eyes to what is objectionable? The concept of loyalty is distorted when it is understood to mean blind acceptance. It is correctly interpreted when it is assumed to cover honest criticism.

A "politicized" world is a world where individual reactions have to be disciplined and subordinated to group interests, and where for that reason, conformism easily becomes an ideal. It is a world where tactics often are given priority over substance and in which, for this reason, we may lose sight of the real interest in our search for propaganda points to be scored. To use a comparison, it is also a world where the preacher may be tempted to give greater effort to winning the approval of the converted than to converting the sinners. If we succumb to such dangers, we lose the ability to communicate our sincere reactions to others who are of a different view, forgetting also how to listen to what they may have to say in explanation of their stands. To the extent that this is permitted to happen, a politicized world becomes a dehumanized world.

. . . We see people trying to find ways to isolate themselves from general trends and to build up closed, protected units. We can understand or even sympathize with such a reaction, but we must recognize that if it represents a resistance to change, it is doomed to failure. Such self-sought isolation may persevere for some time. It will not endure forever, and the longer the change is resisted and adjustment shirked, the more violent will be the final reaction when the walls collapse.

In every society, there is a tendency, as time passes, to lose dynamism and to seek protection behind time-honored formulae, protection against the law of change which is basic to all growth. "Whenever any government," the Virginia Declaration says, "shall be found inadequate or contrary to those purposes, the majority hath an indubitable, inalienable and indefeasible right to reform, alter or abolish it." This is the voice of self-confidence. This is the voice of trust. This is the voice which should always speak in favor of evolution in the interest of man.

A young people, a mature people, knows itself without arrogance or self-infatuation and feels its strength in faithfulness to its inheritance and its characteristics.

. . . Politics in general, and international politics in

particular, were once an area in the main reserved for experts and of comparatively limited significance to the common man. Our time, however, is one of an expansion of politics into increasingly broad areas of common life. This is as true of international politics as of national politics. Anyone who today tries to disengage himself from the political aspects of life cuts himself off from developments of the deepest direct significance for his own destiny.

Mass movements, means of mass communication, pressures of mass interests, the access to new, enormous resources of strength and wealth, together with the rapidity of change, have taken the individual unaware and created situations which he still has to learn how to master.

Difficulty is created by the differences in the scales of values. In the eyes of the East—and perhaps in actual reality—the overwhelming technical progress which is the mark of the West has marked us more than we ourselves realize. The Asian admires the material achievements of the West. He knows what they may mean for the improvement of living conditions in his own world, and he is anxious to make use of these results. But he is not willing to pay for the improvement by changing his way of life in a manner which may seem to him an unavoidable concomitant of technical progress but incompatible with the spirit and traditions of his own people.

As a fruit of the developments which we find below the surface of world events, and also as an ideological inspiration behind those very developments, we meet different attitudes toward the evolution of society and of the world community. Such differences are only too wide and too obvious even among those who share the same fundamental faith in the dignity and worth of men. Let us not overlook the ideological tensions, but let us not exaggerate their significance. Especially, let us not get caught in the belief that divisions of our world between the righteous and the wrongdoers, between idealism and materialism, between freedom and slavery, coincide with national boundaries. The righteous are to be found everywhere—as are the wrongdoers. Those whose only ideal is material well-being meet us in every country—as those whose ideal is selfless service.

In the present world situation, we have had a tendency to give much attention to the need for a wider movement of capital to areas in need of economic development. We are right in doing so. The needs are enormous. But even more important than the money are the skills. The greatest contribution to the creation of the world we want to see is to put at the disposal of the less developed countries our own human resources. Fundamentally, man is the key to our problems, not money. Funds are valuable only when used by trained, experienced and devoted men and women. Such people, on the other hand, can work miracles even with small resources and draw wealth out of a barren land.

The discoveries and inventions which have opened the doors for personal contacts all around the globe have put at our disposal means by which we have unprecedented possibilities to change conditions of life for the better. Our increased knowledge has given us new sources of power and new insight into the nature of disease. It may be that we are still far from mastering disease. It may be that we are still far from mastering the new sources of energy sufficiently well to meet the demand of a quickly growing humanity, for a life in dignity without fear. But, the newly developed perspectives are such that political economy need no longer be the "dismal science" of the days of Malthus.

Thus, in this epoch of change, we see science as a primus motor, we see science also as a human activity, from which we may expect many of the replies to our present-day problems based upon our concepts of man and society.

Many of us have had contact with the European world of the fading nineteenth century—the typical attitudes which have reached far into our own—we have seen the breakdown of the European circle of culture, spiritually, politically, and geographically, and finally, the beginning of a new synthesis on a universal basis. Depending on temperament and background, reactions to this evolution may vary. One may reach back for the imagined calm of the closed world. One may find one's spiritual home in the very disintegration and its drama. Or, one may reach ahead toward the glimpse of the synthesis, inspired by the dream of a new culture in which there is achieved, on a level encompassing the whole world, what once seemed to have become a regional reality in Europe.

He who chooses the latter course will be disappointed, if he believes the task to be easy or the goal close. But he can count on the richest satisfaction in meeting different spiritual traditions and their representatives, if he approaches them on an equal footing and with a common future goal in mind. He will also find rich satisfaction in the progress he will note in the direction of a human community which, while retaining the special character of individuals and groups, has made use of what the various branches of the family of man have attained along different paths over thousands of years.

No diplomat is likely to play the multilateral game well unless he believes in the need for and value of a multilateral approach. No diplomat will adjust himself to this unless he has the courage of his own actions. No diplomat, as a representative in international policy, is likely to meet the demands of public opinion unless he understands and respects this opinion deeply enough to give it leadership. He must feel that this opinion does truly represent the deeper and decisive aspirations in the minds and hearts of the people.

.   .   .   .

The ultimate test of diplomacy is its capacity to evoke a kind of response from the people that will rally public opinion behind what is wise and necessary for the peace and progress of the world.

The spirit and practice of world community must first gain in strength and custom by processes of organic growth. It is to the helping along of these processes of growth that we should devote all our ingenuity and our effort. To the extent that we are able to increase the weight of the common interest as against the weight of special interests, and therefore of the power of the whole community to guide the course of events, we shall be approaching that much nearer to our goals.

No matter what their private judgment, those in positions of authority cannot go against prevailing public opinion or lead in a direction the public is not prepared to follow.

I feel that an administration inspired by sound self-criticism, never blunted by conceit or false loyalties, has a just claim to the respect and confidence of the governments and the public.

The work for security and freedom from fear . . .
will prove hopeless . . . unless peoples and governments alike
are willing to take immediate risks. This will give us a better
chance to avoid the final disaster threatening us if we do not
manage to turn the course of developments in a new direction.

I cannot belong to or join those who believe that our
movement heads toward catastrophe. I believe in growth, a
growth to which we have a responsibility to add our few frac-
tions of an inch.

It is not the facile faith of generations before us who thought
that everything was arranged for the best in the best of worlds
or that physical and psychological development necessarily
worked out toward something they called progress. It is in a
sense a much harder belief—the belief and the faith that the
future will be all right because there will always be enough
people to fight for a decent future.

We are true to this or that ideal, and to this or that interest, because we have in our responsibilities recognized this as an ideal and an interest true to us. We embrace ideals and interests in their own right, not because they are those of our environment. Our relations to our fellow men do not determine our attitudes toward ideals, but are determined by our ideals. If our attitude is consistent, we shall be consistent in our loyalties. If our attitude is confused, then our loyalties will also be divided.

It is easy to say that it is pointless to make a law if it cannot be enforced. However, it should not be forgotten that if a law is the inescapable law of the future, it would be treason not to make it, simply because of the difficulties of the present. Indeed, how could it ever become a living reality if those who are responsible for its development are to succumb to the immediate difficulties? The history of the Jewish people offers some of the most magnificent examples of how ideals and law may be brought to victory through courageous assertion of new universal principles which the wise called folly when they were first introduced in a society shaped on a different pattern.

Who can trace the first sources of a great idea? Such ideas are brought to our awareness when they break through the inertia of human minds and of social institutions. But their antecedents, we find, generally go far back into the past. Early American political philosophy and American liberties were rooted in European theory and in British traditions that dated back in outward expressions to the Great Revolution of 1688. But behind those European theories and behind the British traditions, we find the same ideas, and the prophets for those ideas, in the distant past of our civilization.

Education is not only broad education at the bottom; it is not only school teaching and book learning. It is *civic* education. It is the method by which you bring people not only to national awareness but to the point where they form as free individuals their judgment on political issues. Education is also the method through which you get the doctors, the engineers, the administrators and, to some extent, of course, also the political leaders. However, I do not believe that the universities will be the main breeding ground for political leaders. They are, after all, mostly produced in the field, in practical life.

Between the nation in history and the individual, the family is the primary tie. There is an obvious but subtle interdependence between national and family feelings. It is tempting to speak of them as two phases of the same fundamental reaction. But such a picture does less than justice to a situation in which a feeling for one's forebears gained strength from one's feeling for one's country, and this, in turn, found support in the consciousness of one's origin.

The health and strength of a community depend on every citizen's feeling of solidarity with the other citizens, and on his willingness, in the name of this solidarity, to shoulder his part of the burdens and responsibilities of the community. The same is of course true of humanity as a whole. And just as it cannot be argued that within a community an economic upper class holds its favored position by virtue of greater ability, so it is, of course, impossible to maintain this in regard to nations in their mutual relationships.

· · · ·

I believe that no anthropologist nowadays would say that the various branches of the family of man represent fundamentally different potentialities for contributions and development in various fields of intellectual and material activity. If I may speak on the basis of my own experience, I would say that for my part I have not been able to discover any such differences.

· · · ·

We live in a world where no group can claim superiority in mental gifts and potentialities of development. What may, in practice, seem to point in another direction, is explained by the vast differences which have prevailed in opportunity to bring the gifts to fruition and expression. Those democratic ideals which demand equal opportunities for all should be applied also to peoples and races.

Whatever doubts history may cast, I believe that the hope for a world of peace and order, inspired by respect for man, has never ceased to agitate the minds of men. I believe that it accounts for the great and noble human spirit behind the ravaged exterior of a history whose self-inflicted wounds have become more and more atrocious. And I believe that, at the point we have now reached in our technical development, our creed may gain new possibilities to shape history. A faith like that which has inspired the spiritual life of the West could seem only a dream to the leader of the people of a powerful nation which can dominate others. There is a new situation the day you have to recognize that you cannot dictate to other nations.

Whatever the distance between our goals and the everyday reality we meet around the world, it is not vain to set our targets as they present themselves to the most mature political thinking of our age.

At their best, representatives of our spiritual legacy show the quiet self-assurance of people firmly rooted in their own world. They are, however, at the same time and for that very reason, able to accept and develop a true world citizenship. At their best they are not afraid to like the man in their enemy and they know that such liking gives an insight which is a source of strength. They have learned patience in dealings with mightier powers. They know that their only hope is that justice will prevail and for that reason they like to speak for somebody speaking for justice without humility. They have learned that they can stand strong only if faithful to their own ideals, and they have shown the courage to follow the guidance of those ideals to ends which sometimes, temporarily, have been very bitter. And, finally, their spirit is one of peace.

Poverty is relative. When life has been made safe and elementary needs filled, people are hardly made happier. This is no argument for the contentedness of the poor as it was worshipped in the Victorian fairy-tale world. Nor is it a question of the poverty which is borne with equanimity because it is shared by all. The obligation of all of us is inescapable. It is to raise the living standards for that two-thirds of humanity who live close to the level of starvation or below it. The Buddhist, for instance, is more conscious than we are, of how true it is, even in the most elemental context of everyday life, that man lives not by bread alone.

A needy person, who knows that assistance is given in a spirit of solidarity, knows that he can put it to such use that he will one day be able to repay it even in kind. He may still find difficulty in avoiding a feeling of dependence and a distrust of the motives and attitudes of the helper. This man may also say, "I suppose you realize that it may be more difficult to receive assistance than to give it?"

I had, last year, the privilege of visiting a couple of kibbutzim in Israel and of talking to people coming from many lands, who were devoting their lives to these courageous experiments in practical and total democracy. I looked upon them as fellow workers in an "experiment in progress." Through such experiments alone can progress be achieved.

I also remember experiences of experiments in community development in India. There I met the same enthusiasm, the same devotion, the same idealism as in the kibbutzim. Yet, how different a situation it was! In one case there were people stepping out of their Western societies of highly organized and specialized industrial life, in order to create new collectives, pioneering in the building of a strong economic life on a barren soil. In the other case, communities which, although living in a rich land, had remained poor for lack of revolutionary development. However, the members devoted all their energy toward taking the giant step into the economic and social world of today.

In both cases we meet a realization in practice of basic human rights. The difference, however, indicates the diversity of the problem and this calls for great flexibility in our approach and in the choice of the ways in which the various societies may become integrated into a world community.

The underlying problems now making the Middle East such a troubled area should be understood partly in the terms of which these two experiments in community development may serve as illustrations. They lend special weight to the undertaking of the Member nations in the Charter "to practice tolerance."

We are not what we should be. We have not reached the full strength of our possible contribution, until we have managed to develop within ourselves, and in our relations with others, the sense of belonging. We are no Vatican, we are no republic, we are not outside the world, we are very much in the world. But even within the world, there can be this kind of sense of belonging, this deeper sense of unity. I hope that we are on our road to that sense. I feel that we have moved in that direction and, to the extent that it depends upon me, I can give you one assurance: Whatever I can do for that purpose, I will do.

I hope that from Sweden, and indeed from this university, men and women will go out into the world, not as some kind of missionaries either for the West or for a world community, but in order to serve, by practical work, the evolution toward the synthesis which is on the way.

They can do it, aware of the riches of the cultural heritage which is theirs and of all that Europe stands for. But they should do it in awareness, also, that the best and soundest way to perpetuate this cultural heritage is to meet other peoples and other cultures. This should be done in humble respect for the unique gifts that these men and women, in turn, have offered and still offer to humanity.

Our friends here were singing a Swedish song, the melody of which I think is very beautiful. The words are perhaps a little bit on the sad side. If I may translate the first line of the song, it runs like this: "Will the flowers of joy ever grow?" Those words, in fact, were taken up later by a Swedish poet, who developed the theme in a way which I would like to mention as a kind of background for what I would like to say in conclusion. The poem culminates in the words: "Will the day ever come when joy is great and sorrow is small?"

Looking at it in terms of humanity, looking at it in terms of the development of human society, it can be said, of course, that what we are trying to do here is to make our small contribution, during our short time, to a development which will finally lead us to the day "when joy is great and sorrow is small."

However, you can also look at those words in a much more personal and intimate sense. I think it is possible to interpret them superficially but it is also possible to interpret them in a sense which goes to the very heart of our way of settling our relation to life. And then I would say that on the day we feel that we are living with a duty, well fulfilled and worth our while, on that day joy is great and we can look on sorrow as being small . . .

One of the many contradictions of life is the frequency with which we refer to ourselves as living in a period of change and rapid development. We are so often reluctant to acknowledge the need to adjust our ways to the changes which actually take place.

The ultimate challenge to the political sciences—and to us all—is whether man shall master his world and his history or let himself be mastered by a world and a history which after all is made by man. There cannot be more than one reply to this question. *Man must master his world.* But in order to do so, he must know it.

. . . Manpower and money and education do not mean a thing unless they are given and provided in the right spirit. By the right spirit, I mean such attitudes which reflect an understanding of problems, a sympathetic understanding, neither a feeling of false superiority, nor a feeling of sterile pessimism, nor a feeling of facile optimism. What is needed are realism and understanding.

I know only too well that every real achievement, in whatever field it is, is always the work of many.

Two of our most common human failings seem to be our disrespect for the slow processes of time and our tendency to shift responsibility from ourselves to our institutions. It is too often our habit to see the goal, to declare it and, in declaring it, to assume that we shall automatically achieve it. This leads us to confuse ends with means, to label as failure what is in fact an historic step forward, and in general to mistake the lesser for the greater thing.

We all have a tendency to regard a situation as it exists at any single moment as a lasting one, forgetting that we ourselves and the societies which we form are all subject to the law of change.

It is more difficult to see your brother as a slave or a master. It is easier to see him as somebody with whom you have to live without giving or taking orders. Looking back into the past, we see how peoples have been oppressed—and how peoples have accepted oppression in the name of God. May we not be approaching a time when, in His name, they will instead be giving and accepting freedom?

The relationship of man to society is a relationship for which every generation must seek to find the proper form. But, just as ideas gave direction to the efforts for the best in former times, so direction should be given to those who now carry the responsibility for a sound development of society.

 Part II

NATURE
ART
WRITING
RELIGION

Study the fresh offensive of the birds, the reconnoi-tering of the plover and the maternal heroism of the Ptarmigan when an intruder nears. To harken and to look, to understand and to obey is the way to the familiarity and the affinity which gives the feeling of freedom a solid foundation.

The sunlight plays on its immense instrument of mountain crests and ice expanses, on steeps and valleys.

· · · ·

The grass on the slope was dewy and in the pale twilight it had a nuance of grey.

· · · ·

The gentian, whose flowers in the sunshine had shone with the intense blue color of a spring sky mirrored against the snow, had long since closed its [flower] cups.

. . . .

The mountain crest rose dark from the dead whiteness of the glaciers under a sky deepening into purple, against which the first grey night-clouds already were gathering.

. . . .

The light still plays
   as when a thousand colors play
   in a seemingly colorless, pale
   diamond gem.

. . . .

The sun shines from a clear sky, spreading its rays over the soft grass slopes in the fair, open valley, modelling the structure of the dark southern mountain slopes above, and reflects the polished rocks of the steeper descents where the water flows down.

. . . .

One gets a feeling of fear of the mountain as living nature, and one comprehends the legends about the sleeping giant who sometimes wakes up and shakes himself free of the deviltry that during his sleep has collected in his body.

. . . .

Only when darkness comes does the melody of the brook reach its full strength.

. . . .

Some lines from Knud Rasmussen's translations of Greenlandic poetry come to my mind:

> Oh, summer warmth
> Spreading over the country!
> Not a whiff of wind,
> Not a cloud—
> And between the mountains
> The grazing reindeer
> The dear wilderness
> In the blue distance.

. . . .

The surging rivulet, which earlier glittered brightly in the water around the stones, rises and falls in a murmur. It is noon. Above the ground the air quavers, filled with the clear, spicy fragrance of juniper, dwarf birch, and swamp ground.

. . . .

The night is as moist-shimmering and clear as at the time of the snow-thawing on the plains, and the air has the same cool fragrance of snow water and thawing soil, and the early spring night is filled with the thousand sounds of awakening life.

. . . .

The brook flows easily over a bed of thick moss in a fresh deep-green with nuances in brown. When for a moment the sun is overcast, "the water turns into blood."

. . . .

The grey surface of ice comes to life in its shades—from soiled green to rusty red and the dead tone of ashes, where the mountainside, reflecting the rainy day, turns purple.

. . . .

The rain clouds drift westward after their fruitless attack against the mountain's southern crests, and the entire vast panorama framed within the sunshine-bathed horizon.

Unknown land possesses the temptation of the unknown.

Sarek still possesses the virgin purity that a piece of land keeps only so long as we do not start adjusting it to our comforts—may it be only through paths—with the untidiness and sterilization which seem to be man's eternal follower in nature.

. . . .

Wander into the wilderness where the stillness grows, captures, cleanses, and reforms.

. . . .

It is against the spirit of outdoor life to desire to

travel in luxury even in the regions which have ample space for true mountain sport.

· · · ·

With an increasingly tighter mesh, modern life is caught in a net of stipulations. It is the irony of fate that rules and legislation must be enacted even in order to save the wilderness as a piece of land on which man has not yet put his hallmark. One had hoped that through apperception and feeling for the values in question, unwritten laws would have come into existence.

The silence is broken only by the humming sound of the new snow against the skis. The evening star shimmers as a drop of water. And where it points the way—mile after mile—the mountain land extends still bound by winter but awakening to new adventures of the coming summer.

· · · ·

What is it that gives value to a night like this? Relaxation in solitude, the feeling of vast, untouched nature, and the spell of beauty are the fundamental things.

· · · ·

It is an asset which we cannot afford to lose, to keep a piece of land where we find again "in the dance of buzzing mosquitoes, the time that was before man."

. . . .

At some time all of us need tranquillity and perspective. In the Swedish mountains one achieves solitude and distance, not by fleeing from reality, but by meeting a reality other than that of the workaday world.

. . . .

There is the brook and the vegetation, the dotterel and the reindeer, the sculpture of the mountain-wall, the Laplander and the traveling companion. Truly, existence in the mountains is sufficiently rich to keep us spellbound and to bring us in contact with pulsating life.

. . . .

The long view from the crest or over the moorland, through its simplification of the multitude of bewildering details, gives rest. It forces us to keep our sense of proportion and to feel our smallness and the accidental nature of our existence. Further, it gives a feeling of freedom: the land lies open in front of us, it is ours—by the measure of our ability.

. . . .

The mountain gives a new solitude—in sharing the toil between the path and the climbing, sharing adventure, and experience of beauty. A new solitude is achieved in a camaraderie which it would be difficult to gain in other environments with the same tone of freedom in mutual dependence, of detachment in spite of human contact.

. . . .

The mountain gives us new, rich opportunities to learn to know ourselves. It may expose weaknesses both of mind and body. But it can also give us proof of unexpected resources and, in the words of Rilke, show "our joyful strength which otherwise is concealed."

The deepest understanding of a province belongs to those who spent their childhood there.

I visited Abisko one night around midsummer, when the midnight sun was glowing, the birch leaves new, and shining, and the rhododendron in flower. The willow-warbler was trilling and on the marsh, the breaking ice was moaning. I returned again in the beginning of September when the colors in the many miles of birch woodland started to change and the trees trembled in the mild, moist eastern wind of autumn Lapland.

Traveling the water route between mountains, we get to know the struggle against a nature which, behind the summer brightness, is avaricious and dark.

. . . .

We put on the rucksack and put up with mosquitoes summer after summer because of the great, mellow-sounding effect of nature against which human melodies ring.

. . . .

We are lured by the scent of the birch woodland in the wilderness, the excitement and the triumph of walking the mountain crest, the surging of the rivers in the white nights, the plant life on a southern slope of moorland, and the distant perspective of the sea.

In the morning sun, buttercups formed a golden design against dark slopes in the shade on the other side at the bottom of the valley. But now they too have lost their color. The play of colors during the day has now been followed by the spectrum of a late summer evening.

. . . .

When we reached the altitude of the pass where ice buttercups in the old snow shone white against the charcoal black of the water-soaked earth, the red light of the sunset illuminated the mountain sides ahead of us, at the same time as grey curtains of rain were approaching the valley.

. . . .

Characterized by round hills, the way designed by the mountains spread before us in a blue summer haze. And later on, the sweeping light of the afternoon sun filled the valley below us, caught by the monkshood, and the angelica flowering in the ravines where our way had crossed the rivulets from the high sites of snow on the treeless mountain.

. . . .

Clear melting water drips from green, arched ceilings into the brook, forming the last contribution of the glacier to the heavy mass of water which, milky and frothing, with a color between green and yellow, rushes toward the banks of the delta and the white water mirror.

. . . .

Some strong blasts of wind pull at the stays of the tent. Then silence. And now the rain comes. A rustling in the bushwood, a weak rattle against the taut duck of the tent soon followed by a quick rattling which prevents sleep.

. . . .

A small group of reindeer with year-old calves stands like statues in the shining light against a background of snow and woods—with a shy, somewhat awkward grace which, in reality relieves this typical motif of its picture postcard banality and instead evokes visions of virgin mornings from remote times when life reclaimed the land at the edge of the ice.

. . . .

It is one of those quiet days with low, driving clouds, when light in the moist air becomes a soft silver-tone which subdues and harmonizes the colors, and when it seems as if all sound too has lost its harshness.

. . . .

We bathe at a cape on the shore of which berries shine red against grey stone. On the opposite side of the cape a hawk hovers in the air. From a cove, a sea bird tempts. After a shrill warning suddenly she is silent as some sound from us reaches her. With a metallic ring, small waves lap against the stones.

In the summertime, the way over the moorland reveals a thick carpet of white anemones and dot-plover dance a strange protective dance against intruders.

Mountain flying has no value as a sport. The risks one takes are those of the gambler: the innocent traveler has nothing to say about it, it is not his skill or presence of mind which avoids them. How different it is to personally solve the problem of reconnoitering, of defying bad weather; wading the fjord; finding the right camping site.

To the one who has discovered the mountains, this is a world in which he most easily reaches back to the source and recovers the simplicity and composure of the morning.

Against the midnight sun there is the midwinter darkness, an event as intense as the bright summer nights and more important to those who wish to understand the country and its human problem.

On the steep slopes and oak forests between the dunes, in the spring the soil is white with lilies of the valley. During sunny summer days the air, filled with buzzing insects, quavers hotter and fiercer than anywhere else. The plain lies farther in. On the other side, the sea is grey in fog and rain, but when the sun comes out, richer in color than the Ocean.

. . . .

There are so many ways to get to know a landscape. Some look for the shade beneath the beeches on the crests of the hills. Others seek the trail along the endless shore where the water tempts when the sun is too strong. The abundance of sand carnations or the high white sand lilies may reawaken a botanical interest which had become extinct among the commonplace flora.

See how the summer is reborn and how the spring returns when the way leads up toward fields of snow where ice buttercups are still white in spite of the flybanes already resplendent down in the yellowing birch forest. Follow the tracks of the ice rivers, the delta formation at the river mouth, the retreat of the glacier—all signs of the transformation of the earth itself.

Heidenstam, in a couple of poems in *Thoughts of Solitude,* gave expression to the faithfulness he felt to the roots of his native soil and to the openness to the world outside the borders of his native land.

One of the poems ends with the words:

". . . I desire the soil,
I desire the rocks where as a child I played."

The other poem—also in the form of a confessional—starts:

"Around half the world I have searched
For a spot that most beautiful I could call.
However, so beautiful were they all
That none more beauty than the other had."

.   .   .   .

Our experience of the world's wealth can become the incitement to a new love of our own land.

.   .   .   .

In *Odyssé in the Provinces,* Torsten Fogelqvist says: "First I see the snow clouds clustering around the rhythmic height of Kebnekajse; I see the sandy banks of the Indals River adorned in autumn's golden attire; I see Järvsö blue as a bright spot of light ink. I see Sveg's white smoke in 30° Celsius, and I see strong men in bearskins with icicles in their beards. On the thawing lakes in Dalarna, I hear the ice of spring cracking under the sled runners, and I see the long loads of timber splashing in the golden thaw water of the evening. I see the birches mirrored in the early summer light shimmering over Fryken lakes. I hear the ringing on a holy day from the dusky small churches built in the medieval period. I see the plain of Östergötland in burning sunshine with purling brooks and jubilant larks falling as drops in space. In silence I wander under the stars and fir-trees in the highland woods of Småland. I see Halland's poor ridges as silent melodies—fading away against an agitated autumn ocean. And I see the farmer of Skane standing beside the willow slope or the village pond, brown against the brown dust."

And so—in retrospect, a Swedish traveler summarizes the picture of this rich, changing land which it is our fortune to learn to know and to know.

Art gives more to life than it takes from it.

. . . .

True art does not depend on the reality about which it tells. Its message lies in the new reality which it creates by the way in which it reflects experience.

. . . .

In its search for the basic elements of the world surrounding us and in its fight for mastery of those elements, modern art has revealed to us where lies the real victory of the great artists of the past. Without making us eclectics, it has helped us to understand what has been achieved in the harmony of the best works of the past.

. . . .

Modern art has forged keys to a perfection which it has not itself reached. Shouldering courageously the problems of modern man, reflecting his situation in a world of conflicts born out of his own achievements, it has, thus, earned the recompense of being permitted to illuminate the greatness of man in the high artistic achievements of the past.

. . . .

Modern art teaches us to see, by forcing us to use our senses, our intellect, and our sensibility to follow it on its road of exploration. It makes us seers—seers like Ezra Pound when, in the first of his Pisan Cantos, he senses "The Enormous Tragedy of the Dream in the Peasant's Bent Shoulders." Seers—and explorers—these we must be if we are to prevail.

. . . .

In our minds, we sometimes chisel beauty out of the stone of matter. If we had the courage and perseverance to push these experiences to their extreme point, we would share in the effort of the modern artist to isolate beauty from the impurity of life, even at the cost of dissolving the very forms of life. Why then seeing modern art should we feel estranged when we do not at the first glance recognize the familiar aspects of our everyday world?

One risk, facing equally the worker, the artist, the scientist, and the politician, is the suppression of the inner freedom of the individual through demands for subordination and conformity. There is less tolerance today for the personal, perhaps erratic, experiment in life, than in times which could afford more tolerance. However, the need for such tolerance is as great as ever in the interest of progress and in the interest of peace.

It is a banality . . . to say that the present has given unusual weight to material progress, and that this means that it has deflected interest from spiritual exercises and found ways of satisfying it by a thousand and one new inventions. . . . It may be that the cult of amorphous spontaneity in art and of a philosophy of absurdity will prove to be a transitory phenomenon. No matter what new paths it may open for creative writing, it contains risks of a growing estrangement from readers whose interest is a prerequisite to the continued life of a work of art.

The relationship of a nation—and a generation—to older literature tells something about the continuity of spiritual life. It can also give an idea about the conditions of writing and of the writer: What is the reader seeking, and why?

· · · ·

"A great naturalist guides an author, but a great poet permits the scholar to peer into the secret council chamber of God."

We have tried to conquer time and oblivion by putting our experiences down in words.

We may well feel that there is truth both in the attitude of Schiller and Mann and in the attitude of Carlyle, but that these great authors in their own personalities reveal that the concepts of the nation and of the world, to which they have given expression, are, each one, incomplete and one-sided. Are they not firmly rooted in a national tradition, and yet, do they not belong to all mankind? Are they not internationalists in truth and spirit, and in being so, have they not served their own peoples? The question is not either the nation or the world. It is, rather, how to serve the world by service to the world.

. . . .

In a speech on the 150th anniversary of Schiller's death last spring, Thomas Mann dealt with the conflict between the idea of the world and the idea of the nation as represented respectively by Schiller and Carlyle. He felt that in our time, the narrow field, the nation, was sinking back into the past. Everyone should realize that no problem, be it political or spiritual, could any longer be resolved on the basis of Carlyle's approach. Our world of today, in his view, required a universal vision—indeed, our anguished hearts demanded it. Mankind, as an ideal, was not too weak a guide for our conduct. It was necessary, more necessary than ever, to seek in it an inspiration for all our actions.

T. S. Eliot has spoken of our era as one when wisdom has been forgotten for knowledge and knowledge for information. May we escape the situation where these words become more than an expression of frustration, and where beside esoteric poetry there is produced nothing but literature where realism has been changed into reporting, aimed at filling the mental vacuum of increasing leisure, without worry or effort for the reader.

. . . .

There is one possible reason for the estrangement from the past that is disquieting. In a mass culture, where publicity, working in the interest of sales, is constantly harping on the idea that the latest must be the best, the book becomes relegated to the ranks of disposable and rapidly aging consumer goods. This may lead to an industrialization of literature, which pays attention to the indications about public taste in the bestseller lists in preference to that which is essential and vital. In a situation which is characterized by the quest for novelty and conformism, a weakening of the position of older literature would be natural. The risk is enhanced if, at the same time, the position of the written word becomes more precarious.

The book now has to compete with the press, and jointly, they must hold their own against new forms of expression and communication: the films, radio and television. The need for personal contact with literature of quality reflects an acquired taste. A form of expression requiring less activity on the part of the recipient is favored by that law of least resistance which prevails.

. . . .

In a situation in which dead writers would be definitely forgotten, it is necessary to keep their works alive as a means of inspiring new, creative writing which is begotten in earnest and often born in pain.

The mental climate referred to here is also influenced by political factors. One of these deserves mention. This generation has seen Europe lose much of the powerful position it occupied for centuries, and a wave of nationalism has swept the continents. The revolutionary events we witness have led many into a defeatism which, although unspoken, is revealed by its inseparable companions: fatigue, bitterness, and sterile self-assertion.

There are good reasons, and good chances, to offer resistance to such a situation. The old is not so rotten, nor the new so immature, as many seem to think.

I once knew a man, from Asia, of the highest culture. He told me how, in his early youth, he lived with and loved *The Rubáiyát of Omar Khayyám*. He thought he had made the original text entirely his own, until he came to Britain and became acquainted with Fitzgerald's translation. Then, this in turn became, in the academic surroundings that began to transform him, his "real" *Rubáiyát*. He returned home, however, and again found Omar Khayyám's poems such as he had once made them his own. The pendulum kept swinging, and, he concluded, "Even today I do not know which *Rubáiyát* is mine, Omar's or Fitzgerald's."

The story needs no comment. Figuratively, there are still millions upon millions who do not know which *Rubáiyát* is theirs, Omar's or Fitzgerald's. We must reach the day when they, and all of us, can enjoy, in common, the *Rubáiyát* and the fact that we have it both in Omar's and in Fitzgerald's version.

In his notes on "Nemesis," Linnaeus represented Tradition and our time:

> "Thou sawest my happiness.
> "Thou sawest not goodness.
> "Thou sawest my happiness.

When I was still lying
in darkness,
Thou settest my clock,
Thou cuttest my bread.
So why, almighty Hero,
shouldst Thou forget me now?
My house I have built

by the grace of God.
Therefore, I sleep unafraid."

These lines reverberate with the happy humility before the mystery which from the outset gave his accounts their paean note. Life, to Linnaeus, became a *mysterium tremendum*. It remained, 'til the end, a *mysterium numinosum*.

We have reason to remember the truth that he who fears God will no longer fear men.

Christmas tells us of the redeeming power of true dedication to peace and good will toward men. We are of different creeds and convictions. Events and ideas, which to some of us remain the very basis of our faith, are elements of the spiritual heritage of man which are foreign to others. But common to us all, and above all other convictions, stands the *truth,* once expressed by a Swedish poet when he said that *the greatest prayer of man does not ask for victory but for peace.*

I remember the words of Tao Tse-Tung. "Heaven arms with pity those whom it would not see destroyed."

Over the ages and over the continents, these words join with those of the Psalmist: "There is Mercy with Thee; therefore shalt Thou be Feared."

In the Sermon on the Mount, it is said that we should take no thought of the morrow—"for the morrow shall take thought for the things of itself. Sufficient unto the day is the evil thereof." Can anything seem farther from the practical planning, the long-term considerations typical of political life? And yet—is this not the very expression of the kind of patience we must all learn to show in our work for peace and justice?

Wonderment at nature's proof of the Lord's omnipotence had made young Linnaeus write this comment on his first experience of the midnight sun: "Oh Lord, Thy verdicts are incomprehensible." Later, when his eye, guided by somber experiences, was directed toward the world of men, this wonderment was turned into fatalistic mysticism. Suffice it to say that Linnaeus, even in the darker reaches of his being, carried out the role as one of those in whom people had wished to see their features reflected with particular clarity.

Even the notes on Nemesis, now all too inaccessible, belong to our living literature. Crime and retribution, misfortune breeding misfortune, the vanity of mundane aspirations—thus fate is linked to fate in his dance of death, where the style has the economy and dry precision of a woodcut. Linnaeus' introductory words, addressed to his only son, provide the motif of these pictures of life. "There was a time when I doubted that God cared about me; many years have taught me what I leave to you. Everyone wants to be happy, but few are able to be." Besides this, however, there is a poem where brooding finally gives way to the trust of a grown-up child.

In a televised interview some time ago, a youngster of sixteen asked me, with concern, why there is no reference to God in the United Nations Charter. In my reply, I drew his attention to the Preamble of the Charter where the nations express their "faith in the dignity and worth of the human person" and pledge themselves "to practice tolerance and live together in peace with one another as good neighbors." I felt sure that he saw here an expression of what was recognized as the will of God: that we should love our neighbors as ourselves.

For the Christian faith, "the Cross is that place at the center of the world's history . . . where all men and all nations, without exception, stand revealed as enemies of God . . . and yet, where all men stand revealed as beloved of God, precious in God's sight." So understood, the Cross should not separate those of Christian faith from others. It should, instead, be that element in their lives which enables them to stretch out their hands to peoples of other creeds in the feeling of universal brotherhood.

Faith is a state of the mind and the soul. In this sense we can understand the words of the Spanish mystic, St. John of the Cross: "Faith is the union of God with the soul."

From scholars and clergymen on my mother's side I inherited a belief, that, in the very radical sense of the Gospels, all men were equals as children of God, and should be met and treated by us as our masters in God.

. . . .

The language of religion is a set of formulas which register a basic spiritual experience. It must not be regarded as describing, in terms to be defined by philosophy, the reality which is accessible to our sense and which we can analyze with the tools of logic. I was late in understanding what this meant. When I finally reached that point, the beliefs with which I was once brought up and which, in fact, had given my life direction even while my intellect still challenged their validity, were recognized by me as mine in their own right and by my free choice. I feel that I can endorse those convictions without any compromise with the demands of that intellectual honesty which is the very key to maturity of mind.

. . . .

The two ideals which dominated my childhood world met me fully harmonized and adjusted to the demands of our world of today in the ethics of Albert Schweitzer, where the ideal of service is supported by and supports the basic attitude to man set forth in the Gospels. In his work I also found a key for modern man to the world of the Gospels.

The Churches are guardians of and spokesmen for the deepest beliefs and the loftiest dreams of man.

. . . .

In speaking for justice, truth and trust in public affairs, the Churches may be a decisive force for good in international and national political life. Should the Churches go any further? In my view, there is one thing they could do. They could help to explain how world affairs are run and what is the responsibility of every one of us. In doing so, they could help to explain what an organization like the United Nations stands for: how its ideals run parallel to the very aims and beliefs of the common man who wishes to live in peace with his neighbors, with freedom to build his own little world in human dignity.

. . . .

A war to be fought in the hearts of men can be waged only by those speaking directly to men. It is here that I see the great, the overwhelming task of the Churches and of all men of good will of every creed in the work for peace. Their vital contribution to this work is to fight for an ever wider recognition of their own ideals of justice and truth.

 # Part III

THE WORLD'S CONDITION

Part III

THE WORLD'S CREATION

The history of mankind is made by men, but men partly make it blindly. No one can foresee with certainty what will emerge from the give-and-take of the forces at work in any age. History often seems to run its course beyond the reach of any man or nation.

Perhaps a future generation, knowing the outcome of our present efforts, will look at them with some irony. They will see where we fumbled and they will find it difficult to understand why we did not see the direction more clearly and work more consistently toward the target it indicated. So it will always be, but let us hope that they will not find any reason to criticize us because of a lack of that combination of steadfastness of purpose and flexibility of approach which alone can guarantee that the possibilities which we are exploring will have been tested to the full.

. . . It is for society to shoulder its responsibility in the fight against poverty, disease, inequality and lack of freedom, by the means put at its disposal by science and technology. It is, likewise, the duty of society to shoulder the responsibility for the development of ways in which men can live together in this shrunken world, turning the dynamics of change into the stability of peace.

A nation seeks its image in fiction and in history. Seeks and forms. Finds and forms itself accordingly—or rejects.

Time is a great healer and "playing for time" is an important element in the tactics we must follow in these days of crisis, anxiety and frustration.

Just as we cannot shape our world at will like a handful of clay, neither do pressures and events inexorably lead on to a preordained doom. They are subject to influence and change.

In the classical Chinese collection of poetic philosophy, ascribed to Tao Tse-Tung, it is said somewhere that whoever wants to grip the world and shape it will fail, because the world is a spiritual thing that cannot be shaped.

Often in history, situations have arisen where people could neither live together nor fight each other. In spite of this, the world has moved on and the situation of despair has become past history.

. . . It has been said that I am interested in mountaineering. That's true. However, the qualities this requires are just those which I feel we all need today: perseverance and patience, a firm grip on realities, careful but imaginative planning, a clear awareness of the dangers but also of the fact that fate is what we make it and that the safest climber is he who never questions his ability to overcome all difficulties.

Although perhaps profiting from wider support of the common man than did our predecessors, we have to work in a much harsher climate. Where our predecessors dreamed of a new heaven, our greatest hope is that we may be permitted to save the old earth. Behind that hope, however, are now rallied all peoples of the world.

Deep-rooted conflicts which have run their course all through history, and seemed to reach a new culmination before and during the Second World War, continue. And destructive forces which have always been with us make themselves felt in new forms. They represent, now as before, the greatest challenge man has to face.

Those people and nations which are to live together in the future, if we succeed in overcoming the immediate risks of war, will not be of the same generation as those who do not see any possibility of living together as they are now and as conditions are today.

Our time is basically characterized by two movements in civilization—one toward greater social justice *within*
nations, and the other toward greater political and economic
equality and justice *between* nations.

. . . It appears evident that no nation or group of
nations can base its future on a claim of supremacy. It is in its
own interest that the other groups have opportunities equal to
those it has had itself. To contribute to this is an act of solidarity
which is not only good for the whole but, in the long run, re-
dounds to the advantage even of those who take the action. It
means that leadership is substituted for power—leadership both
in giving other peoples their chance and in assisting them, without issuing commands, to find the best way to develop their
spiritual and material resources.

Every nation has its heroes, its martyrs and its saints. The world also has its heroes and saints. One who long ago spoke among a small, oppressed people for the brotherhood of all men was sacrificed as a danger to the safety of his own nation. Western civilization has aspired for nearly 2,000 years to follow the life and teachings of this apostle of peace. But all through those 2,000 years, nationalism, in the narrow and dangerous sense of the word, has remained a major force. In the light of history, one might well ascribe to mankind the words of Milton's Lucifer: "For only in destroying, I find ease to my relentless thoughts."

A nationalism which seeks its own gratification at the expense of others, or which aims at increased power or territorial expansion, definitely reveals itself as an expression for social ambitions which we must overcome.

. . . A national feeling can be harmoniously merged with a feeling of international responsibility.

The reply to nationalists who wish to remain aloof in such vain efforts at self-protection, is that the way to safeguard what they rightly want to defend is not isolation. The way is a vigorous and self-confident development, in free contact with the world, of the special qualities and assets of their nation and their people—a development which should give them their just weight in the international balance. Giving thus to the world what is specifically ours, we could manifest and protect our national character, while accepting change and opening our minds to the influences of the world.

To this day there is much talk about a new nationalism. First of all it refers to the deep and strong current which carries the freedom movement of the Asiatic and African people. Sometimes in such discussions a tone of critical superiority is heard which is not limited to the primitive or immature expressions of this current itself but even considers the basic attitude naïve and obsolete. Against the new nationalism, there is talk about a new internationalism, characterized by a consciousness of all that unites people and nations, regardless of race, history, ideology or economic conditions. Trying to maintain that such a contrasting situation exists is superficial and unjust. It is as unfair as the tendencies to ridicule the spirit which inspired our national renaissance during the final decades of the 19th century.

We live in a period of fundamental and rapid changes in the relationship of nations and peoples having differing cultures and social systems. The new age that is emerging is an age of promise. It could also become one of disaster. We are seeking to cope with world issues of great difficulty but equally of high challenge. The hope of finding peaceful, just and constructive solutions of these issues rests upon our ability to foster the growth of understanding, cooperation, and mutual accommodation of interests among all the nations.

Look anywhere in the world today. Is there any solution in sight except peacefully negotiated agreements? Granted, at a given moment, the prospect for such agreements seem dim indeed. What is the alternative? Only the attempt to establish "one world" by force of arms. And that is no alternative. Such an attempt would lead to a catastrophe just as fatal to the presumed victor, as to the vanquished. I believe this should be recognized as true, no matter on what ideology you base your judgment and for whatever way of life you plead.

Nation borders on nation, peoples get in touch with each other, and whatever differences there may exist and whatever conflicts of interests the people may see, they are forced to live together, fighting or in peace. As neighbors, with limits put by nature to their possible self-sufficiency, there is a need to develop forms for international intercourse, permitting more or less highly developed degrees of cooperation. So an institutional system of coexistence is developed with its rules and practices.

Only those who do not want to see can deny that we are moving these days in the direction of a new community of nations, however far we may be from its full realization, however often we may seem to have chosen the wrong path, however numerous the setbacks and disappointments have been.

Society is welded together by the higher "reason," common to us all, which is the bearer of justice.

We can understand faith in a "supranational" justice, through which may be created an international *Civitas Legum*. In attempting to interpret internationalism, this seems to me to be the key. *Civitas Dei* was a dream of the past. The present-day attempts to form an international organization with common executive organs had not yet begun. Instead, there is a glimpse here of a world society, where national states live under the protection of an internationalism which gains its strength from the very logic of justice itself, not from dictates of power, and in which, therefore, the only international organs needed are of a judicial nature.

They are lost who do not face the basic facts of international interdependence.

They are lost who permit defeats to scare them back to a starting point of narrow nationalism.

They are lost who are so scared by a defeat as to despair about the future. For all of them dark prophecies may be justified.

We have a long road ahead of us to traverse before nations can hope to eliminate the threat of atomic destruction. But we cannot hope to travel at all unless we begin to take down the barriers to understanding and friendship and begin to work together in growing confidence.

To some, the word "tolerance" may sound strange in a time of "Cold War" and of negotiations "from positions of strength." It may have an overtone of meekness or appeasement. And yet, have we reason to believe that what was true in the past is no longer true? It is not the weak but the strong who practice tolerance. The strong do not weaken their position in showing tolerance. On the contrary, only through tolerance can they justify their strength in the face of those counteracting forces that their own strength automatically sets in motion.

I am sure that this holds true of all those in the present world situation, who consider themselves to be "strong" countries, be it the Powers whose military resources give them key positions, or those who have achieved a state of democracy and of recognition of human rights.

I think that we all can recognize that the effort to strike a delicate balance between news and undramatic diplomacy in the stories we have to tell is something that comes close to what I call "diplomatic back-seat driving." I think that the phrase expresses my whole idea. We have all had the pleasure of having back-seat drivers, and we all know for that reason what the feelings may be of those who are at the wheel. That does not mean that those in the back seat may not be very wise, may not have the right to claim the fullest understanding of the one at the wheel; but one should realize that, in diplomacy and in politics, the one in the back seat sees less of the road than the one at the wheel. I mention this because it has, over the years, developed into a problem of my life.

History places a burden on our shoulders. The creative urges of the emergent nations are tinged with strong emotions from the past. It is for all of us, denying neither the good nor the ills of that past, to look ahead and not permit old conflicts to envenom the spirit of the creative work before us.

The technique of war has been revolutionized in a way which now brings with it destruction of vast areas, death to millions upon millions of the civilian population, and economic and financial ruin with effects lasting over long periods after the fighting stops. All this does not mean that our ancestors in Benjamin Franklin's time were necessarily more civilized than we. However, the technique of war today presents a new problem to civilized man. To the diplomat of the middle of the twentieth century, war is something that must be averted at almost any cost.

One consequence of the basic approach in the unfolding events of the nineteenth century was that contact with the Asian and African peoples did not break down the closed character of Western European culture. Other peoples were approached from points of departure which made it very difficult to assimilate what they, in turn, had to offer. The ethnologist, the geographer or the religious scholar could impart his findings, but largely these remained exotic information, of interest to experts alone, not integrated into the mainstream of culture. Such integration is difficult in any case. In this setting, it was made almost impossible. To make it a reality required an intellectual humility and an open-minded set of values, which came about only when European man was shaken in his self-confidence and saw the walls around his closed world crumble before the pressures of new forces which Europe itself in large part had called into being. . . . What strikes one in the first place, perhaps, is how much they did not see and did not hear, and how even their most positive attempts at entering into a world of different thoughts and emotions were colored by an unthinking, self-assured superiority.

. . . .

In today's perspective, the Europe of the early nineteenth century appears as a tightly closed cultural world, highly developed but essentially regional in character. Goethe's "universality" was combined with a firm conviction of the supremacy of the European man of culture, a supremacy which erected invisible walls around his spiritual life in relation to other parts of the world.

As time went on and the military and political influence of Europe was extended further and further in Asia and Africa, this conviction of supremacy found increasingly concrete—and increasingly simple—expressions. In many cases, it came to be represented by persons whose only superiority over those they had to deal with lay in the power they had back of them. Nobody should minimize the admirable achievements frequently attained by the colonizers of the nineteenth century. But nobody should forget that colonization reflected a basic approach which may have been well founded in certain limited respects, but which often mirrored false claims, particularly when it touched on spiritual development. Applied generally, it was untenable.

The motto of one of the old ruling houses in Europe was: "I serve." This must be the guiding principle, and also the inspiration and the challenge, for all those who have to carry the responsibility of office for any community. Is it not natural that this motto should be felt with special faith, sincerity and loyalty by those who assist in the greatest venture in international cooperation on which mankind has ever embarked?

At the induction in my present office, I quoted these lines by a Swedish poet: "The greatest prayer of man is not for victory, but for peace."

. . . I have repeatedly quoted a phrase coined by Paul Valéry (*"Ceux qui préfèrent se noyer à nager dans les conditions de l'eau"*). It expresses the simple truth that, when trying to change our world, we have to face it as it is.

It seems to me that the basic movements of our time, the peaceful democratic evolution and the peaceful achievement of independence, should not be confused with their various manifestations—war, revolution, dictatorship.

In the pride of self-realization, natural to new states, we should welcome the constructive element—a self-assertion like that of a young man coming of age, conscious of his powers, eager to find his own way, to make his voice heard and to render his contribution to progress. We should meet this new enthusiasm with understanding, in full appreciation of the rich gifts it may bring to a world of many nations and peoples in friendly competition. In world affairs, such an attitude, which is in line with the great tradition of this country, may be regarded as an expression of true democracy in international life.

. . . One is often asked whether this Conference has any political significance. In its conception, its purposes and its approach, this Conference is as nonpolitical as a conference of this nature should be. The personalities that we see around us are not concerned with expediency, with strategy or with tactics of any kind, but with the search for truth and with the idea of brotherhood based on the concept that all knowledge is universal. Nevertheless, since their deliberations are bound to affect human life in all its aspects, it would not be correct to say that they have no political significance. I am sure that their cooperation will ease tensions. I am sure that their exchange of scientific data will inspire confidence and I am sure that the trend of their discussions will turn men's thoughts away from war to peace. We all should render our thanks to the scientists who, by moving in this direction, will expiate, on behalf of all of us, that feeling of guilt which has so universally been felt, that man in his folly should have thought of no better use of a great discovery than to manufacture the deadliest instruments of annihilation.

The intricate web of relationships which now exists has, as part of its basis, the new means of communication which has overnight made our world so much smaller than it was in previous generations. We are all very conscious of the fact that it is now but a question of hours for military forces to reach distant parts of the globe and that the old considerations of strategy, based on geographic separation, no longer count for much.

News also reaches us from all corners of the globe, almost as quickly as if we had been eyewitnesses. We are parties to an action practically at the very moment it is undertaken. The nerve signals from a wound are felt at once all through the body of mankind.

We meet in a time of peace which is no peace, in a time of technical achievement which threatens its own masters with destruction.

We meet in a time when the ideas evoked in our minds by the term "humanity" have switched to a turbulent political reality from the hopeful dreams of our predecessors.

The widening of our political horizons to embrace, in a new sense, the whole of the world, should have meant an approach to the ideal sung in Schiller's "Ode to Joy," but it has, paradoxically, led to new conflicts and to new difficulties in establishing simple human contact and communication.

There are difficulties explained by the fact that we are still very close to the epoch when the West lived happily in its feeling of superiority. For an Asian or an African, it may be difficult to enjoy the spiritual heritage of the West, without a sense of cleavage, which may be pushed all the way to rootlessness, or without an uneasiness, while the Westerner may widen his cultural range and absorb other traditions without corresponding tensions.

My African friends, you can learn from mistakes in other parts of the world, in other phases of history. I think that you will see that what is needed is unity with diversity, diversity respected within the framework of an even deeper respect for unity. You can create, and I know you will create, the African personality as part of the picture of mankind today. But I know that, in doing so, you will preserve all the richness you have inherited; each group, each people within this continent.

The very study of disarmament, may be the vehicle for progress toward greater international political understanding. That is to say, disarmament is never solely the result of the political situation, it is also partly instrumental in creating the political situation.

In the international field, there is a need for practical action, for helping under-developed countries to achieve such economic progress that will give them their proper share in the wealth of the world. There is also a need for political arrangements, providing a framework for a development in peace toward independence and self-determination for peoples now experiencing a revival of national pride and achieving political maturity. But there is also a need for inspiration, for the creation of a spirit among the leaders of the peoples to help them use the forces which they have to master, for peace and not for war, for evolution and not for revolution.

The best effort in the direction of peace is frustrated, when you meet and have to face an atmosphere where people simply believe that the movement is in the opposite direction.

Men organize themselves into families. The families join together in villages or tribes. The tribes and the villages fuse into peoples, and one day, out of the self-consciousness of a people, there develops a feeling of difference and separateness, the positive expression of which is a feeling of nationhood. The nation organizes its life within a set of constitutional rules, evolving in practice or crystallized as law. Under the constitution, the people develop national organs with different functions and a division of responsibilities representing a balance of power. Through those organs, laws are given, setting the pattern for the lives and activities of the individuals and the groups which constitute the nation.

We have seen how, out of present-day conflicts and the underlying tensions, has grown a widespread state of fear and frustration, of distrust and desperation. This is in itself a source of evil. It maintains an atmosphere in which unbalanced reactions may suddenly release the explosive power of the forces which we have to master.

Our country, with its shortcomings and merits, is a small part of the big world. There is no necessity for comparison with other countries in order to fully appreciate our own. It has a tradition that does not disclaim self-effacement, which is considered enlightened but actually is provincial as opposed to earlier romantic self-exaltation, but it has no understanding for the self-praise which only exposes an inner insecurity.

Working at the edge of the development of human society is to work on the brink of the unknown. Much of what is done will one day prove to have been of little avail. That is no excuse for the failure to act in accordance with our best understanding, in recognition of its limits but with faith in the ultimate result of the creative evolution in which it is our privilege to cooperate.

 Part IV

UNITED NATIONS

Part IV

UNITED NATIONS

We all have within us a center of stillness surrounded by silence.

This house, dedicated to work and debate in the service of peace, should have one room dedicated to silence in the outward sense and stillness in the inner sense.

It has been the aim to create in this small room a place where the doors may be open to the infinite lands of thought and prayer.

People of many faiths will meet here, and for that reason none of the symbols to which we are accustomed in our meditation could be used.

. . . .

However, there are simple things which speak to us all with the same language. We have sought for such things and we believe that we have found them in the shaft of light, striking the shimmering surface of solid rock.

. . . .

So, in the middle of the room, we see a symbol of how, daily, the light of the skies gives life to the earth on which we stand, a symbol to many of us of how the light of the spirit gives life to matter.

. . . .

But the stone in the middle of the room has more to tell us. We may see it as an altar, empty not because there is no God, not because it is an altar to an unknown god, but because it is dedicated to the God whom man worships under many names and in many forms.

. . . .

The stone in the middle of the room reminds us also of the firm and permanent, in a world of movement and change. The block of iron ore has the weight and solidity of the everlasting. It is a reminder of that cornerstone of endurance and faith on which all human endeavor must be based.

. . . .

The material of the stone leads our thoughts to the necessity for choice between destruction and construction, between war and peace. Of iron, man has forged his swords, of iron, he has also made his plowshares. Of iron, he has constructed tanks, but of iron he has likewise built homes for man. The block of iron ore is part of the wealth we have inherited on this earth of ours. How are we to use it?

. . . .

The shaft of light strikes the stone in a room of utter simplicity. There are no other symbols, there is nothing to distract our attention or to break in on the stillness within ourselves. When our eyes travel from these symbols to the front wall, they meet a simple pattern, opening up the room to the harmony, freedom and balance of space.

. . . .

There is an ancient saying that the sense of a vessel is not in its shell but in the void. So it is with this room. It is for those who come here to fill the void with what they find in their center of stillness.

The founding fathers of this great nation took upon themselves the responsibility for the creation of a new and independent state on American soil. They did so in a firm trust in the future and with a firm belief in the basic decency of man. In that spirit, they managed to weld together, in one nation, people from many nations of the world. *"E pluribus unum"* is rightly inscribed on the shield of the United States.

That could also be the motto of the United Nations in its defiance of seemingly insuperable difficulties, in its belief in freedom and in its hope for world unity. Read in the right spirit, the Charter of the United Nations expresses an approach to the political problems of man which would have been well understood by men like Jefferson and Lincoln.

It is a true measure of the leadership and idealism of Woodrow Wilson that it is not a vain pastime to give some thought to the question of how he would have looked at our endeavors, our failures and our successes, in the fields to which he devoted the best of his life. He is not only the first and foremost spokesman for true international organization, he is one of those who helped to create an international conscience which is, and will remain, a living force in all attempts to build a world of order.

No state, no group of states, no world organization, can grip the world and shape it, either by force, or by any formula of words in a charter or a treaty. There are no absolute answers to the agonies and searchings of our time.

We may well rejoice in having taken the first steps

toward the establishment of an international democracy of
peoples, bringing all nations—irrespective of history, size or
wealth—together on an equal basis as partners, in the vast venture of creating a true world community. But we have taken
only the first steps, and they have often proved painful. There
is a maturity of mind required of those who give up rights.
There is a maturity of mind required of those who acquire new
rights. Let us hope that, to an increasing extent, the necessary
spiritual qualities will be shown on all sides.

The essence of international service will expose us to
conflicts. It will not permit us to live lazily under the protection
of inherited and conventional ideas. Intellectually and morally,
international service therefore requires courage to admit that you
are wrong, even in the face of a weaker adversary, and courage
to defend what is your conviction even when you are facing the
threats of powerful opponents. But while such an outlook exposes us to conflicts, it also provides us with a source of inner
security; for it will give us "self-respect for our shelter."

I personally believe that just as negotiation keeps people from shooting, in the same way, reasonable progress toward a goal keeps people from rushing into a conflict because they cannot get everything at once or cannot get it in just the form that they would like.

In other words, the two lines of preventive action which I think are obviously indicated, are, first, to stabilize the situation in the field on a day-to-day basis and to avoid the incidents which may lead to major frictions. Secondly, to be quietly helpful by being a third party, with which the two conflicting parties can discuss matters which may help them to bridge the gulf by working out a maximum of understanding.

It is true we are passing through a period of unusual threats to human society and to peace. The dangers are too well known for me to add any comments here. If anything, you hear and see too much about them in the headlines of every paper. It is also true that the role of the Organization is necessarily a modest one, subordinated as it must be to governments, and through governments to the will of the peoples.

· · · ·

Although the dangers may be great and although

our role may be modest, we can feel that the work of the Organization is the means through which we all, jointly, can work so as to reduce the dangers. It would be too dramatic to talk about our task as one of waging a war for peace, but it is quite realistic to look at it as an essential and—within its limits—effective work for building dams against the floods of disintegration and violence.

The United Nations is an expression of our will to find a synthesis between the nation and the world. It is an attempt to provide us with a framework, inside which it is possible to serve the world by serving our nation, and to serve our nation by serving the world. Whatever may be the past shortcomings of this experiment in world organization, it gives sense and direction to the efforts of all men who are striving toward a better world. The Organization was born out of the cataclysms of the Second World War. It should justify the sacrifices of all fighters for freedom and justice in that war. I remember the bitter lines of a great Anglo-American poet [Annette Kohn] who writes in an "Epitaph for the Unknown Soldier":

"To save your world, you asked this man to die,
  Would this man, could he see you now, ask why?"

It is our duty to the past, and it is our duty to the future, so to serve both our nations and the world as to be able to give a reply to that anguished question.

The many who, together, form this Organization—peoples, governments and individuals—share one great responsibility. Future generations may come to say of us that we never achieved what we set out to do. May they never be entitled to say that we failed because we lacked faith or permitted narrow self-interest to distort our efforts.

We often hear it said that the United Nations has succeeded here, or has failed there. What do we mean? Do we refer to the purposes of the Charter? They are expressions of universally shared ideals which cannot fail us, though we, alas, often fail them. Or do we think of the institutions of the United Nations? They are our tools. We fashioned them. We use them. It is our responsibility to remedy any flaws that may be in them. It is our responsibility to correct any failures in our use of them. And we must expect the responsibility for remedying the flaws and correcting the failures to go on and on, as long as human beings are imperfect and human institutions likewise.

The United Nations cannot lay down the law within any national community. Those laws have to be established in accordance with the will of the people, as expressed in the forms indicated by their chosen constitution. But just as the United Nations can promote peace, so it can, in joint deliberations, define the goals of human rights which should be the laws of the future in each nation.

The United Nations is only a first approximation to the world order which we need and which one day must be brought about. It is in the field of international politics something like Niels Bohr's model or the atom in the field of nuclear physics. It is not the final reply. It is not even a tentative reply which, though incomplete, is correct in its details. It is a reply which, if properly understood and developed, provides an approach, leading us ahead, step by step, on the long road toward a satisfactory solution.

The work of today within and for the United Nations is a work through which the basis may be laid for increasingly satisfactory forms of international cooperation and for a future international system of law and order, for which the world is not yet ripe.

Faith and Order are words which serve as a motto for the United Nations in its international activity. The Organization is animated by Faith in the dignity and worth of men, born equal. It must serve and strengthen Order as a guarantee for peace, giving to everyone a possibility to live a full life of freedom.

.   .   .   .

The United Nations must recognize and respect all the different creeds and attitudes represented by its Member nations.

It stands outside all confessions but it is, nevertheless, an instrument of faith. As such, it is inspired by what unites and not by what divides the great religions of the world.

It has been said that one should never forget that the United Nations operates in a glass house. I would add that in our world of today, it could not operate properly under any other conditions; in fact, in my view, it *should* operate in a glass house in order to serve its purposes. Multilateral diplomacy is, by its very nature, such that secrecy has lost its place and justification.

The international civil servant, who works for an organization made up of members of different ideologies and interests, remains under the obligation that applies to all of us— to be faithful to truth as he understands it. In doing so he is loyal—both in relation to the organization and to his country.

. . . .

At this time of great ideological conflicts and violent clashes of interests, technological and economic developments have, as never before, brought us together as members of one human family. We are unified beyond race or creed on a shrinking globe, in face of dangers of our own making. In such a situation, many ethical problems take on a new significance and our need to give sense to our lives exceeds the inherited standards. True, our duties to our families, our neighbors, our countries, our creeds have not changed. But something has been added. This is a duty to what I should call international service, with a claim on our lives equal to that of the duty to serve within those smaller units whose walls are now breaking down. The international service of which I speak is not the special obligation, nor the privilege, of those working in international economic corporations, in the field of diplomacy, or in international political organizations. It has become today the obligation, as well as the privilege, of all.

. . . .

International service requires of all of us first and foremost the courage to be ourselves. In other words, it requires that we should be true to none other than our ideals and interests. But these should be such as we can fully endorse after having opened our minds, with great honesty, to the many voices of the world.

. . . .

Nobody should use his position in an international organization for attacks on his own country or its policies, however strongly he may feel that he is right. Nor should anybody, as a national, attack the international organization for which he is working, and thereby place himself outside the discipline and the procedure established for the maintenance of that organization. But it is equally true that nobody should suffer, either as a national, or in his position in the international organization, for faithfulness to ideals of truth and justice, provided he observes the laws of his country as well as of the organization which he serves.

In the United Nations Secretariat, we have nearly sixty different nationalities represented. None of us can make ourselves entirely free from our own background, and why should we? Is not the national accent and the national experience very often a great asset in international cooperation? It certainly is. At the same time, it may introduce an element of division. It may tend to split, what should be a unity, into separate compartments. For the Secretary-General of the United Nations and his collaborators, it is necessary to find ways to make the national elements an asset. It is necessary to overcome the divisive influences. It is necessary to try to create a unity in which the diversity of the national backgrounds is fully respected and preserved. This should be done in such a way as to be an asset, rather than a liability in the work.

      The Secretariat has an essential part to play in the world affairs of today. We will play it if we accept the price for building up our position of strength. We must reject a role of insignificance which is subject to constant criticism. We must reject shirking the risks of a full part in our world. We must choose a role of responsibility and independence, sacrificing part of the illusory safety one may derive from a locked door.

The United Nations finds itself in a difficult stage of its development. It is still too weak to provide the security desired by all, while being strong enough and alive enough, effectively, to point out the direction in which the solution must be sought. In its present phase, the Organization may look to many like a preacher who cannot impose the law he states, or realize the gospel he interprets. It is understandable if those who have this impression turn away in distrust or with cynical criticism, forgetting that setbacks, in efforts to implement an ideal, do not prove that the ideal is wrong. Also, it is forgotten that, at the beginning of great changes in human society, there must always be a stage of frailty or seeming inconsistency.

It may be said of the United Nations that what is required from the governments and people is a renewed faith, a faith renewed every day, expressed in a never abandoned, every day newly initiated, responsible action for peace.

I would be the last to minimize the very great difficulties which lie in the way of governmental steps which are necessary to translate the will to peace into concrete progress toward peaceful solutions. These difficulties must nevertheless be surmounted. The United Nations cannot, and of course should not, attempt to do this alone. The governments with which the power of decision rests may not be able to do it alone. But the governments, strengthened by the help available from and within the United Nations, can, and I hope will, decide to lead their people, step by step, upon this road toward a more secure and promising future for them all.

The principles of the United Nations Charter are, by far, greater than the Organization in which they are embodied, and the aims, which they are to safeguard, are holier than the policies of any single nation or people. As a servant of the Organization, the Secretary-General has the duty to maintain his usefulness by avoiding public stands on conflicts between Member nations, unless and until such an action might help to resolve the conflict. However, the discretion and impartiality thus imposed on the Secretary-General, by the character of his immediate task, may not degenerate into a policy of expediency. He must also be a servant of the principles of the Charter, and its aims must ultimately determine what for him is right and wrong. For that he must stand. A Secretary-General cannot serve on any other assumption than that all Member nations honor their pledge to observe all articles of the Charter—within the necessary limits of human frailty and honest differences of opinion. He should also be able to assume that those organs which are charged with the task of upholding the Charter will be in a position to fulfill their task.

When I think of the work before us . . . I am reminded of a famous idea of Dostoevsky in *The Brothers Karamazov,* where he has one of his heroes say that the future may be one of a struggle between the State trying to make itself Church and the Church trying to make itself State.

Applied in international life today, we might say that the United Nations represents ideals at least professed by all nations. But, it is not a super-state trying to impose on people any "right" way of life or any way of life different from one freely chosen by the people. On the contrary, it seeks to penetrate the life of states in their international relations and to influence their conduct toward a wider realization of those ideals.

•　•　•　•

The United Nations is in tune with the basic movements of our time. All its pledges and all its work are in the direction of peaceful progress toward greater social justice within nations and greater political and economic equality and justice between nations.

But . . . the United Nations has no power to encroach upon the national sovereignty of any state against the will of its government and people. It would indeed be against the letter and the spirit of the Charter for the United Nations to attempt to impose its will in domestic matters.

Is not an experiment something tentative and passing? And should not the United Nations be regarded as something definite and lasting? I think it is important to be clear on this point. Certainly the experiences and achievements of the United Nations, as it is today, are helping us to build the future. The United Nations is something definite also in the sense that the concepts and ideals it represents, like the needs it tries to meet, will remain an ineluctable element of the world picture. However, that does not mean that the present embodiment of the groping efforts of mankind toward an organized world community represents a definite shape for all time. The United Nations is, and should be a living, evolving, experimental institution. If it should ever cease to be so, it should be revolutionized or swept aside for a new approach.

The United Nations is an organization for continuous diplomatic negotiations concerning concrete political issues, providing also for international administrative action in the economic and social fields.

Economic burdens and restrictions on freedom of action of any nation are imposed not by the United Nations, but by the facts of international life and the national interests of the countries concerned. Programs of economic and military aid, and the conferences and negotiations through which agreements are sought, are undertaken by governments because they are deemed to be necessary to the national interest and position of the countries concerned and not because of restrictions imposed from outside by charters and treaties.

Public debate, in the United Nations, is dominated

by the same differences among the parties as international political life as a whole. But behind closed doors these differences
are diluted. The human factor carries more weight there, and
confidential exchanges are possible even across frontiers which
otherwise appear impassable.

It has so often been said that the world of today is
one which requires organized international cooperation on a
basis of universality that one repeats it with hesitation. However, there are reasons to do so. It still seems sometimes to be
forgotten that—whatever views may be held about the United
Nations as an institution—the principle of organized international cooperation on a basis of universality, which is reflected
in the Organization, is one which has emerged from bitter
experiences and should now be considered as firmly established.

The United Nations is part of the great pattern of
change of our time. It functions as a tool in the hands of governments and peoples, and of individuals, in their effort to give
to that change a constructive direction. The Organization is

based on the recognition of the fundamental unity of all mankind in its interest in peace and in progress based on justice and freedom. Its basic idea is not one of an enforced unity with a deadening subordination of the nation, the group or the individual under a global pattern. The concept which it reflects is what an American scientist once characterized in some words about the unity of science. He said that this unity is "far more a unity of comparable dedication than a unity of common, total understanding." He continued: "This heartening phrase, the unity of science, often tends to evoke a wholly false picture, a picture of a few basic truths, a few critical technical methods and ideas, from which all discoveries and understanding of science derive; a sort of central exchange, access to which will illuminate the atoms and the galaxies, the genes and the sense organs. . . . The history of science is rich in examples of the fruitfulness of bringing two sets of techniques, two sets of ideas, developed in separate contexts for the pursuit of new truth, into touch with one another. The sciences fertilize each other; they grow by contact and by common enterprise. Once again this means that the scientists may profit from learning about any other science . . . It means that the unity is a potential unity, a unity of the things that might be brought together and might throw light, one on the other. It is not global or total or hierarchical."

·   ·   ·   ·

These words about the unity of science are, I believe, profoundly true about all those human activities which create society and determine human relations. Especially do I know that they apply to the interests and activities which are brought together within the sphere of the United Nations. If the United Nations is to succeed in giving to the development of the world all that this experiment in organized coexistence can yield, it will be on the basis of a recognition of our fundamental unity, in the sense described in this quotation, and through the devoted efforts of men, who dare to be pioneers in their field of activity and who dare to risk "a fruitful mistake" in their effort to meet the challenges of an ever-widening knowledge and of ever-widening—but also ever more complex—human relationships.

Our world of change is one in which only those who show this intellectual and moral courage—and who are free to exercise it—will be able to face the challenge of the future.

When I asked for the privilege of exercising my right of reply at this stage of the general debate, it was not because I wanted to use this opportunity to correct any factual mistakes or misrepresentations. That should be unnecessary in the light of the very full debates in the Security Council and at the very recent emergency special session. . . .

My reason for taking the floor now is another one. I felt that, before the debate goes any further, it would be appropriate for me to make clear to the Assembly certain respects on which the Secretary-General has been addressed by some speakers.

In those respects, the General Assembly is facing a question not of any specific actions but of the principles guiding United Nations activities. In those respects, it is a question not of a man but of an institution.

Just one week ago the General Assembly adopted a resolution regarding the Congo operation. It did so after a thorough debate and a full presentation of facts. As that is the situation, it may well be asked why those same facts should now be brought out again in the Assembly as a basis for new and far-reaching conclusions, perhaps involving even a question of confidence.

The question before the General Assembly is no longer one of certain actions but one of the principles guiding them. Time and again the United Nations has had to face situations in which a wrong move might have tended to throw the weight of the Organization over in favor of this or that specific party in a conflict of a primarily domestic character. To permit that to happen is indeed to intervene in domestic affairs contrary to the letter and the spirit of the Charter.

To avoid doing so is to be true to the letter and spirit of the Charter, whatever disappointment it might cause those who might have thought that they could add to their political weight by drawing the United Nations over to their side.

The Head of the Soviet Delegation to the General Assembly, this morning, in exercising his right of reply, said, among many other things, that the present Secretary-General has always been biased against the socialist countries, that he has used the United Nations in support of the colonial powers fighting the Congolese Government and Parliament in order to impose "a new yoke on the Congo," and finally, that if I, myself, and I quote, "do not muster up enough courage to resign, so to say in a chivalrous manner, then the Soviet Union will draw the necessary conclusions from the obtained situation." In support of this challenge, the representative of the Soviet Union said that it is not proper for a man who has "flouted elementary justice to hold such an important post as that of the Secretary-General." And later on he found reason to say to the delegates of this session that they should not "submit to the clamorous phrases pronounced here" by me "in attempts to justify the bloody crimes perpetrated against the Congolese people."

The General Assembly can rightly expect an immediate reply from my side to a statement so directly addressed to me and regarding a matter of such potential significance.

The Assembly has witnessed over the last weeks how historical truth is established; once an allegation has been repeated a few times, it is no longer an allegation, it is an established fact, even if no evidence has been brought out in order to support it. However, facts are facts, and the true facts are there for whosoever cares for truth. Those who invoke history will certainly be heard by history. And they will have to accept its verdict as it will be pronounced on the basis of the facts by men free of mind and firm in their conviction that only on a scrutiny of truth can a future of peace be built.

I have no reason to defend myself or my colleagues against the accusations and judgments to which you have listened. Let me say only this, that you, all of you, are the judges. No single party can claim that authority. I am sure you will be guided by truth and justice. In particular, let those who know what the United Nations has done and is doing in the Congo, and those who are not pursuing aims proper only to themselves, pass judgment on our actions there. Let the countries who have liberated themselves in the last fifteen years speak for themselves.

I regret that the intervention to which I have found it necessary to reply has again tended to personalize an issue which, as I have said, in my view is not a question of a man but of an institution. The man does not count, the institution does. A weak or nonexisting executive would mean that the United Nations would no longer be able to serve as an effective instrument for active protection of the interests of those many Members who need such protection. The man holding the responsibility as chief executive should leave if he weakens the executive; he should stay if this is necessary for its maintenance. This, and only this, seems to me to be the substantive criterion that has to be applied.

I said the other day that I would not wish to continue to serve as Secretary-General one day longer than such continued service was, and was considered to be, in the best interest of the Organization. The statement this morning seems to indicate that the Soviet Union finds it impossible to work with the present Secretary-General. This may seem to provide a strong reason why I should resign. However, the Soviet Union has also made it clear that, if the present Secretary-General were to resign now, they would not wish to elect a new incumbent but insist on an arrangement which—and this is my firm conviction based on broad experience—would make it impossible to maintain an effective executive. By resigning, I would, therefore, at the present difficult and dangerous juncture, throw the Organization to the winds. I have no right to do so because I have a responsibility to all those States Members for which the Organization is of decisive importance, a responsibility which overrides all other considerations.

It is not the Soviet Union or, indeed, any other big powers who need the United Nations for their protection; it is all the others. In this sense the Organization is first of all their Organization, and I deeply believe in the wisdom with which they will be able to use it and guide it. I shall remain in my post during the term of my office as a servant of the Organization in the interest of all those other nations, as long as they wish me to do so.

In this context the representative of the Soviet Union spoke of courage. It is very easy to resign; it is not so easy to stay on. It is very easy to bow to the wish of a big power. It is another matter to resist. As is well known to all members of this Assembly, I have done so before on many occasions and in many directions. If it is the wish of those nations who see in the Organization their best protection in the present world, I shall now do so again.

This is, of course, the basic reason for the principle spelled out at the very first stage of the Congo operation, and approved by the Security Council, to the effect that the United Nations Force is not under the orders of a government requesting its assistance and cannot be permitted to become a party to any internal conflict, be it one in which the government is engaged or not. It is common experience that nothing, in the heat of emotion, is regarded as more partial than when one takes himself the position of a party of strict impartiality.

Further, as I have said, this is a question not of a man but of an institution. Use whatever words you like, independence, impartiality, objectivity—they all describe essential aspects of what, without exception, must be the attitude of the Secretary-General. Such an attitude, which has found its clear and decisive expression in Article 100 of the Charter, may at any stage become an obstacle for those who work for certain political aims which would be better served or more easily achieved if the Secretary-General compromised with this attitude. But if he did, how gravely he would then betray the trust of all those for whom the strict maintenance of such an attitude is their best protection in the world-wide fight for power and influence.

Thus, if the office of the Secretary-General becomes a stumbling block for anyone, be it an individual, a group or a government, because the incumbent stands by the basic principle which must guide his whole activity, and if, for that reason, he comes under criticism, such criticism strikes at the very office and the concepts on which it is based. I would rather see that office break on strict adherence to the principle of independence, impartiality and objectivity than drift on the basis of compromise. That is the choice daily facing the Secretary-General. It is also the choice now openly facing the General Assembly, both in substance and in form. I believe that all those whose interests are safeguarded by the United Nations will realize that the choice is not one of the convenience of the moment but one which is decisive for the future, their future.

One last word. Sometimes one gets the impression that the Congo operation is looked at as being in the hands of the Secretary-General, as somehow distinct from the United Nations. No: This is your operation, gentlemen. And this is true whether you represent the African and Asian member countries, which carry the main burden for the Force and for its Command, or speak and act for other parts of the world. There is nothing in the Charter which puts responsibility of this kind on the shoulders of the Secretary-General or makes him the independent master of such an operation. It was the Security Council which, without any dissenting vote, gave this mandate to the Secretary-General on July 14. It was the Security Council which, on July 22, commended his report on the principles that should be applied. It was the Security Council on August 9, which, again without any dissenting vote, confirmed the authority given to the Secretary-General. Again, just a week ago, the General Assembly, without any dissenting vote, requested the Secretary-General to continue to take vigorous action. Indeed, as I said, this is your operation, gentlemen. It is for you to indicate what you want to have done. As the agent of the Organization,

I am grateful for any positive advice, but if no such positive advice is forthcoming—as happened in the Security Council on August 21, when my line of implementation had been challenged from outside—then I have no choice but to follow my own conviction, guided by the principles to which I have just referred.

It is essential for the growth of a human society in which the dignity of the human being will be respected, that every effort is made to make the step in the direction of an organized world community a success. In these circumstances I may be excused if I express the deepest worry at seeing the way in which this Organization is abused in words, and abused as an instrument for purposes contrary to the Charter.

It is understandable that staff members should sometime feel frustrated and even depressed. In that, they are not different from their fellow beings in other positions who are influenced by the trend of world events. There is only one answer to the human problem involved, and that is for all to maintain their professional pride, their sense of purpose, and their confidence in the higher destiny of the Organization itself, by keeping to the highest standards of personal integrity in their conduct as international civil servants and in the quality of the work that they turn out on behalf of the Organization. This is the way to defend what they believe in and to strengthen this Organization as an instrument of peace for which they wish to work. Dejection and despair lead to defeatism—and defeat.

We have been accused of servility in relation to the West, of softness in relation to the East, of supporting this or that man in the Congo whom one group or another on the world scene has chosen to make its symbol, or for assisting another man to whom another group has chosen to tie its hopes for the success of interests it wishes to safeguard. However, this is no excessive price to be paid for avoiding the thing for which no one in my position should be forgiven: to compromise, in any political interest, with the aims and principles of this Organization. It has not been done and it will not be done with my knowledge or acquiescence. I can only repeat what I said in the General Assembly that I would rather see the office of the Secretary-General break on this principle than drift on compromise. May these observations be accepted as a reply to the criticism of the Secretariat which we find repeated in the Soviet statement, and also as a reply to all those who now criticize us so freely for the very opposite reasons.

All the misunderstandings, all the willful misrepresentations, all the efforts to make what is done now suspected, could be treated lightly as a part of a political game in which, I believe, the players themselves must regard all these various statements only as moves and not as statements of fact, if it were not for their effect on this Organization and its authority.

The end of all political effort must be the well-being of the individual in a life of safety and freedom. The means to this end are the independence, peace, integrity and prosperity of the country. In turn, this goal requires the maintenance and progress of economic life, the functioning of a good judiciary system, a soundly working administration, all under the responsibility of a government, stable, thanks to its firm roots, in the free will of the people. This is the perspective in which the effort of the United Nations must be seen. This perspective should determine our judgment and give us the sense of proportion necessary if we are to avoid substituting the means for the ends and the interests of the man or the group for those of the people.

I believe, and many believe with me, that this Organization in all its frailty represents the sole approach which may give us a chance to reduce the risk that the constant frictions, large and small, which characterize the life of our present-day world, build up to a tension easily triggered into a clash in which we would all be engulfed.

On the seas we sail, we have to face all the storms and stresses created by the ideological, economic, and social conditions of our world. We have to meet the impatience of those sailors who expect land on the horizon tomorrow, also the cynicism or sense of futility of those who would give up and leave us drifting impotently. On the shores, we have all those who are against the whole expedition, who seem to take a special delight in blaming the storms on the ship instead of the weather.

When Beethoven's *Ninth Symphony* opens, we enter a drama full of harsh conflict and dark threats. But the composer leads us on, and in the beginning of the last movement we hear again the various themes repeated, now as a bridge toward a final synthesis. A moment of silence and a new theme is introduced, the theme of reconciliation and joy in reconciliation. A human voice is raised in rejection of all that has preceded and we enter the dreamt kingdom of peace. New voices join the first and mix in a jubilant assertion of life and all that it gives us when we meet it, joined in faith and human solidarity.

On his road from conflict and emotion to reconciliation in this final hymn of praise, Beethoven has given us a confession and a credo which we, who work within and for this Organization, may well make our own. We take part in the continuous fight between conflicting interests and ideologies which so far has marked the history of mankind, but we may never lose our faith that the first movements one day will be followed by the fourth movement. In that faith we strive to bring order and purity into chaos and anarchy. Inspired by that faith we try to impose the laws of the human mind and of the integrity of the human will on the dramatic evolution in which we are all engaged and in which we all carry our responsibility.

· · · ·

The road of Beethoven in his *Ninth Symphony* is also the road followed by the authors of the Preamble of the Charter. It begins with the recognition of the threat under which we all live, speaking as it does of the need to save succeeding generations from the scourge of war which has brought untold sorrow to mankind. It moves on to a reaffirmation of faith in the dignity and worth of the human person. And it ends with the promise to practice tolerance and live together in peace with one another as good neighbors and to unite our strength to maintain peace.

. . . .

Experience has shown how far we are from the end which inspired the Charter. We are indeed still in the first movements. But no matter how deep the shadows may be, how sharp the conflicts, how tense the mistrust effected in what is said and done in our world of today we are not permitted to forget that we have too much in common, too great a sharing of interests, and too much that we might lose together, ever to weaken in our efforts to surmount the difficulties. We must turn the simple human values, which are our common heritage, into the firm foundation on which we may unite our strength and live together in peace.

May the symphony develop its themes, uniting us in its recognition of fear and its confession of faith.

❧ Sources

page 18 Last speech before Secretariat Staff of the United Nations, New York, New York, September 8, 1961

page 19 Speech before World Council of Churches, Evanston, Illinois, August 20, 1954

page 19 Speech at Johns Hopkins University, Baltimore, Maryland, June 14, 1955

pages 20–21 Speech before Swedish Tourist Association, Stockholm, Sweden, February 27, 1960

page 21 Edited from material written for "This I Believe," radio program, 1954

page 22 Speech at Cambridge University, Cambridge, England, June 5, 1958

page 22 Speech before World Council of Churches, Evanston, Illinois, August 20, 1954

pages 22–23 Speech to American Association for the United Nations, New York, New York, September 14, 1953

page 23 University of Lund, Lund, Sweden, May 4, 1959

pages 23–24 Edited from material written for "This I Believe," radio program, 1954

pages 24–27 Inaugural Address, Swedish Academy, Stockholm, Sweden, December 20, 1954

page 27 Edited from material written for "This I Believe," radio program, 1954

pages 27–28 Speech at International Airport, New York, New York, April 9, 1953

page 28 Speech at Johns Hopkins University, Baltimore, Maryland, June 14, 1955

page 28 Introduction to the Annual Report of the United Nations, 1960–61, New York, New York, August 17, 1961

page 29 American Jewish Committee, New York, New York, April 10, 1957

page 29 Discussion at Williamsburg, Virginia, May 14, 1956

pages 30–31 American Jewish Committee, New York, New York, April 10, 1957

page 31 Discussion at Williamsburg, Virginia, May 14, 1956

page 31 American Jewish Committee, New York, New York, April 10, 1957

page 32 Discussion at Williamsburg, Virginia, May 14, 1956

pages 32–33 Speech at Cambridge University, Cambridge, England, June 5, 1958

page 33 Speech at Johns Hopkins University, Baltimore, Maryland, June 14, 1955

pages 33–34 Speech at Atoms for Peace Award Ceremony, Rockefeller Institute, New York, New York, January 29, 1959 *page 34* Speech before Swedish Tourist Association, Stockholm, Sweden, February 27, 1960

pages 34–35 Speech at Johns Hopkins University, Baltimore, Maryland, June 14, 1955

pages 35–36 Governors' Conference, Miami, Florida, May 19, 1958

page 36 Stanford University, Palo Alto, California, June 19, 1955

page 37 Discussion at Williamsburg, Virginia, May 14, 1956

page 37 Speech before Swedish Tourist Association, Stockholm, Sweden, February 27, 1960

pages 37–38 Governors' Conference, Miami, Florida, May 19, 1958

page 38 Speech at Atoms for Peace Award Ceremony, Rockefeller Institute, New York, New York, January 29, 1959

pages 38–39 University of Lund, Lund, Sweden, May 4, 1959

page 39 Speech before World Council of Churches, Evanston, Illinois, August 20, 1954

page 40 International Law Association, McGill University, Montreal, Canada, May 30, 1956

pages 40–41 Speech at Atoms for Peace Award Ceremony, Rockefeller Institute, New York, New York, January 29, 1959

pages 41–42 University of Lund, Lund, Sweden, May 4, 1959

page 42 Foreign Policy Association Dinner, New York, New York, October 21, 1953

pages 42–43 Speech at New York University, New York, New York, May 20, 1956

page 43 Speech at New York University, New York, New York, September 14, 1953

page 43 Speech at International Airport, New York, New York, April 9, 1953

page 44 American Jewish Committee, New York, New York, April 10, 1957

page 44 University of Lund, Lund, Sweden, May 4, 1959

page 45 Speech at Johns Hopkins University, Baltimore, Maryland, June 14, 1955

page 45 American Jewish Committee, New York, New York, April 10, 1957

page 46 Discussion at Williamsburg, Virginia, May 14, 1956

page 46 Press Conference, New York, New York, February 4, 1960

page 47 Inaugural Address, Swedish Academy, Stockholm, Sweden, December 20, 1954

pages 47–48 University of Lund, Lund, Sweden, May 4, 1959

page 48 Stanford University, Palo Alto, California, June 19, 1955

page 49 American Jewish Committee, New York, New York, April 10, 1957

page 49 Upsala College, East Orange, New Jersey, June 4, 1956

page 75 Speech at Atoms for Peace Award Ceremony, Rockefeller Institute, New York, New York, January 29, 1959

page 76 Annual Meeting of Swedish Academy, Stockholm, Sweden, December 20, 1957

page 77 At Four Camping Sites

pages 77-78 Stanford University, Palo Alto, California, June 19, 1955

pages 78-79 Annual Meeting of Swedish Academy, Stockholm, Sweden, December 20, 1957

pages 79-80 University of Lund, Lund, Sweden, May 4, 1959

pages 80-81 Annual Meeting of Swedish Academy, Stockholm, Sweden, December 20, 1957

page 81 Speech before World Council of Churches, Evanston, Illinois, August 20, 1954

page 81 Speech before Plenary Session, General Assembly, United Nations, New York, New York, April 10, 1953

page 82 American Jewish Committee, New York, New York, April 10, 1957

page 82 Speech before World Council of Churches, Evanston, Illinois, August 20, 1954

pages 82-83 Annual Meeting of Swedish Academy, Stockholm, Sweden, December 20, 1957

pages 83-84 Speech before World Council of Churches, Evanston, Illinois, August 20, 1954

page 85 Edited from material written for "This I Believe," radio program, 1954

page 86 Speech before World Council of Churches, Evanston, Illinois, August 20, 1954

page 89 Speech at New York University, New York, New York, September 14, 1953

pages 89-90 University of Chicago, Chicago, Illinois, May 1, 1960

page 90 Speech at Atoms for Peace Award Ceremony, Rockefeller Institute, New York, New York, January 29, 1959

page 90 Annual Meeting of Swedish Academy, Stockholm, Sweden, December 20, 1957

page 91 Speech at New York University, New York, New York, May 20, 1956

page 91 Speech at New York University, New York, New York, September 14, 1953

page 92 Speech before World Council of Churches, Evanston, Illinois, August 20, 1954

page 92 Speech at International Airport, New York, New York, April 9, 1953

page 107   Foreign Policy Association Dinner, New York, New York, October 21, 1953

page 108   Speech at Cambridge University, Cambridge, England, June 5, 1958

page 108   University of Lund, Lund, Sweden, May 4, 1959

page 109   University Institute of Somalia, Mogadiscio, January 14, 1960

page 109   Press Conference, May 19, 1955

page 110   Speech before World Council of Churches, Evanston, Illinois, August 20, 1954

page 110   Extemporaneous discussion at United Nations Correspondents Association luncheon, New York, New York, September 10, 1959

page 111   University of Chicago, Chicago, Illinois, May 1, 1960

page 111   Speech before World Council of Churches, Evanston, Illinois, August 20, 1954

page 112   Task and Responsibility

page 112   University of Chicago, Chicago, Illinois, May 1, 1960

pages 115–117   Leaflet written by Hammarskjöld, dedicated to the Meditation Room of the United Nations, New York, New York, 1957

page 117   Speech at New York University, New York, New York, September 14, 1953

page 118   Speech at New York University, New York, New York, May 20, 1956

page 118   Speech at New York University, New York, New York, September 14, 1953

pages 118–119   Speech at Cambridge University, Cambridge, England, June 5, 1958

page 119   Speech at Johns Hopkins University, Baltimore, Maryland, June 14, 1955

page 120   Press Conference, February 27, 1956

pages 120–121   Last speech before Secretariat Staff of the United Nations, New York, New York, September 8, 1961

page 121   Stanford University, Palo Alto, California, June 19, 1955

page 122   Statement before the General Assembly, New York, New York, September 26, 1957

page 122   Speech at New York University, New York, New York, May 20, 1956

page 123   American Jewish Committee, New York, New York, April 10, 1957

page 123   Speech at Atoms for Peace Award Ceremony, Rockefeller Institute, New York, New York, January 29, 1959

page 124   Report to General Assembly, United Nations, New York, New York, August 22, 1959

page 143 Speech before the General Assembly, United Nations, New New York, December 7, 1960

page 143 Speech before the General Assembly, United Nations, New York, New York, October 17, 1960

page 144 Speech before the Security Council, United Nations, New York, New York, December 7, 1960

page 144 Speech to American Association for the United Nations, New York, New York, September 14, 1953

pages 145–146 Speech on United Nations Day, New York, New York, October 24, 1960